INCREDIBLE

ART

Sue Nicholson
Deri Robins
Fiona Macdonald

Silver Dolphin

San Diego, California

Silver Dolphin Books
An imprint of the Advantage Publishers Group
10350 Barnes Canyon Road, San Diego, CA 92121
SilverDolphin www.silverdolphinbooks.com

ISBN-13: 978-1-59223-943-6
ISBN-10: 1-59223-943-9

Printed and bound in China
1 2 3 4 5 12 11 10 09 08

Conceived, edited and designed by QED Publishing
A Quarto Group Company
226 City Road, London EC1V 2IT
www.qed-publishing.co.uk

Written by Sue Nicholson and Deri Robins
Artwork by Melanie Grimshaw and Sarah Morley
Photography by Michael Wicks

Publisher: Steve Evans
Creative Director: Zeta Davies
Senior Editor: Hannah Ray

Web site information is correct at the time of going to press.
However, the publishers cannot accept liability for any
information or links found on third-party Web sites.

Picture credits
Key: t=top, b=bottom, r=right, l=left, c=center
The Art Archive/ Eileen Tweedy, Tate Gallery, London 88 tl/
Musée des Art Africains et Océaniens/Dagli Orti/ 143 tr/ 154 tr,
156 t and c, 158 tr and br, 162 cr and br, 172 tr, 174 tr;
Corbis/ Rune Hellestad 31 bl/ Douglas Kirkland 42 tl/ Roger
De'La Harpe, Gallo Images 98 bl/ Caroline Penn 136 tl/ Kevin
Fleming 149 tl/ Richard Cummings 152 tr;
Corbis/Christie's Images/ Dave G. Houser 160 r/ Robert Holmes
165 tc/ 166 tr/ Reza Webistan 170 r/ 176br;
Getty Images/ Steve Bly/Stone 145 br/ Bridgeman Art Library
147 cl;
Japan National Tourist Organisation/ 168 r;
Royal Ontario Museum/ Dinodia 165 tl and c, 166 b;
Travelsite/ Neil Setchfield 139 tl, 141 c;
Werner Forman/ British Museum 151 tl.

The words in **bold** are explained
in the glossary on page 236.

2

Contents

Contents, continued

WORLD ART

COLLAGE, SCULPTURE, AND SPECIAL EFFECTS

Colored pencils

Drawing and cartooning kit

Anyone can create great drawings and cartoons—it's just a matter of learning how to look! But to get started, you'll need an art kit.

Start with a few basic materials: a pad of paper, a couple of pencils, and a pencil sharpener. As you learn more, you can try some of the other materials below. Any extra bits and pieces are listed with each project.

Pencils

You need at least three types of pencils: 2H (a hard pencil, for sharp lines and details), HB (medium hard, for sketching), and 2B (a soft pencil, for drawing guidelines and for **shading**). The 4B to 8B pencils are very soft, and are for dark shading.

Eraser

Not just for deleting: you can use it to make **highlights** in your drawings by revealing the paper underneath.

Charcoal and chalk

Charcoal and **chalk** are great for quick sketches, for large areas of color, and for adding **texture**.

Oil or chalk pastels

Chalk pastels are soft and crumbly and give a delicate, blurry effect when you smudge them. Oil pastels make brighter colors.

Pens and felt-tips

These are perfect for strong black lines or sharp details. The **nibs** come in many different sizes—you need some thick ones and some thin ones. Colored felt-tip pens are good for coloring cartoons.

Wax crayons

These are inexpensive and are good for making bold, colorful pictures and **resist work**.

Paints and inks

You can use poster paints and inks for making bold, colorful cartoons. **Watercolors** are good for soft colors. Remember, if you use paint or ink, draw your outlines in waterproof pen or they will run when you start painting.

Paper

Use scrap paper for your rough ideas and save your best paper for your final drawings. Smooth **sketch paper** is good for pencil and pen drawings. Rough **construction paper** is ideal for pastels, chalk, crayons, and charcoal. Experiment with different types, sizes, and colors of paper.

Take care!
Some projects involve cutting, gluing, or spraying. Always ask an adult for help when you see this sign.

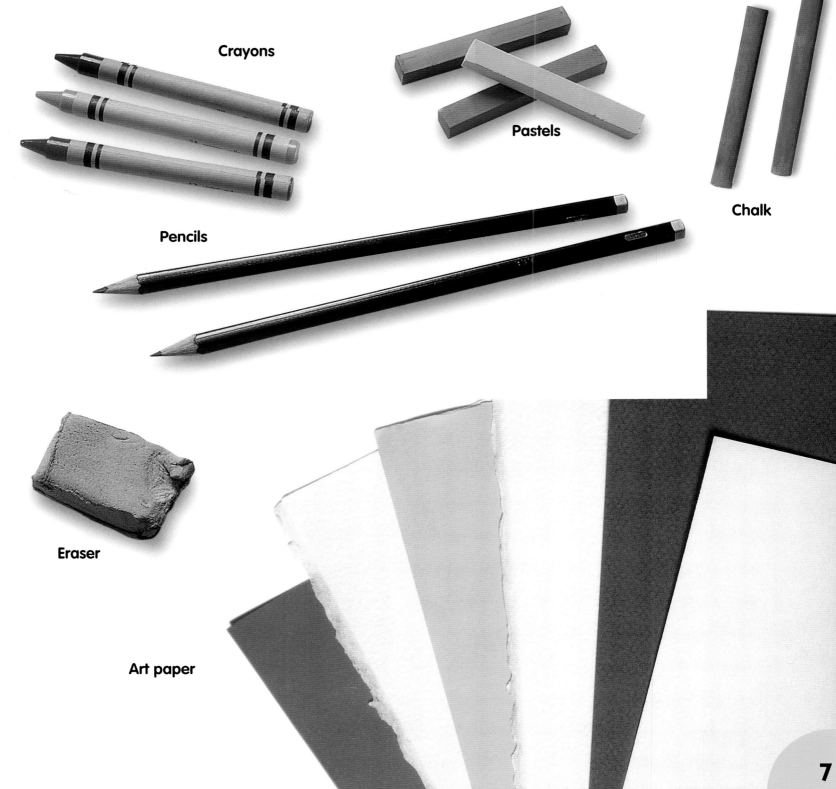

Crayons

Pastels

Chalk

Pencils

Eraser

Art paper

Drawing people

When you draw people, start with simple shapes such as ovals, circles, and oblongs.

1 Draw an oval for the head at the top of your paper.

2 Add a tube for the neck. Make it almost as wide as the head.

Me and my grandma

Draw a picture of yourself with someone special— a brother, sister, grandparent, or best friend.

Remember to build up the bodies with circles and ovals. Make the shapes light, so you can erase them later.

3 Add a large oval for the top part of the body and a smaller oval for the hips.

4 Draw circles for the shoulders, oblong shapes for the upper arms, more circles for the elbows, and oblongs for the lower parts of the arms.

5 Add the legs in the same way. Make the ovals wider at the top. Add circles for knees, then thinner oblong shapes for the shins.

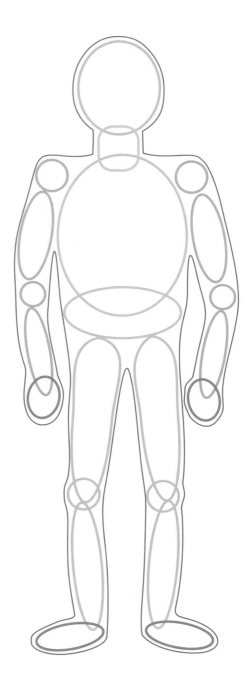

6 Add simple hand and feet shapes, then finish off with the body's **outline**.

Top tip
Find photos or cut pictures of people out of magazines. Practice drawing their bodies by using simple shapes.

Drawing movement

Here's how to make a cardboard figure to help you draw people in different positions.

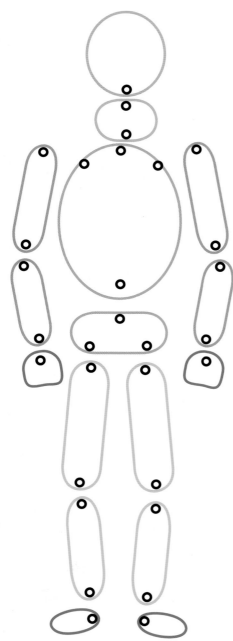

Trace these shapes onto tracing paper, then white cardboard

1 Trace the shapes on the left onto tracing paper, then transfer them to cardboard.

2 Using safety scissors, cut out the cardboard shapes. Push a small hole in each shape with the tip of a ballpoint pen and fasten the shapes together with paper fasteners.

3 Move the parts of your cardboard body so that it looks like it is running, jumping, or kicking a ball.

4 Use the figure to help you draw body shapes in different positions, or trace around the figure.

speed lines

Speed lines will help bring your moving body to life.

You will need:

- Tracing paper
- White cardboard
- Paper fasteners

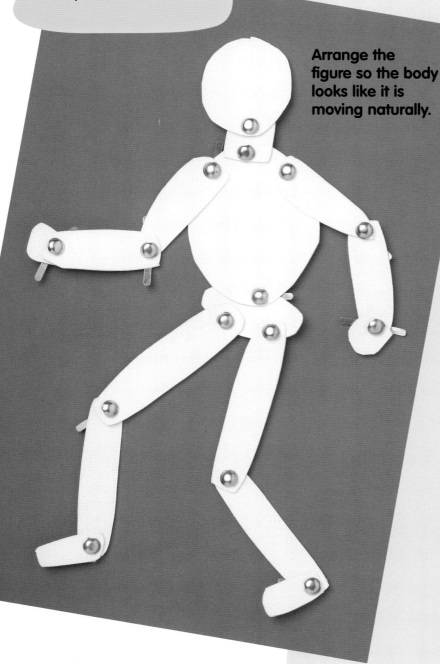

Arrange the figure so the body looks like it is moving naturally.

If you add straight speed lines, the figure will look as if it is flashing past you.

If you add curved speed lines, the figure will look as if it is twirling or twisting around.

Click for Art!

To see how artists have drawn moving bodies, go to **www.artlex.com.** Click on "Mol–MZ" and scroll down to "movement" or "motion."

11

Furry animals

You can draw animals in the same way as people, using simple shapes such as circles, ovals, and triangles.

Top tip
Real animals are hard to draw because they never keep still! Collect animal pictures in a scrapbook so you can look carefully at the animals' shapes.

1 Draw simple shapes such as circles and ovals first. Make sure the animal's head is smaller than its body.

2 Draw an outline around the shapes. Erase lines you no longer need.

3 Add details such as the ears, eyes, nose, and whiskers.

Drawing fur

To make animals look lifelike, you need to draw the texture of their fur. Here are some different ways.

Velvety-smooth fur drawn with a soft brown oil pastel

Short, spiked fur drawn with a fine felt-tip pen

Soft, fluffy fur drawn with oil pastel

Shaggy fur drawn with scribbled pencil lines

Click for Art!

For animal drawings by Beatrix Potter, go to **www.peterrabbit.co.uk/beatrixpotter/beatrixpotter1c_a.cfm.** For an outline drawing of a wolf, go to **www.tate.org.uk/collection/** and search for "Henri Gaudier-Brzeska" and "A Wolf."

Here are some other furry animals for you to sketch.

4 Add color and texture for the fur. See "Drawing fur" on page 12 for tips on drawing different types of fur.

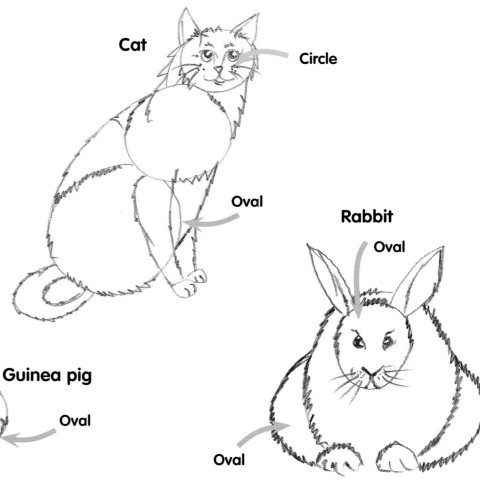

Cat
Circle
Oval

Rabbit
Oval
Oval

Guinea pig
Oval
Circle

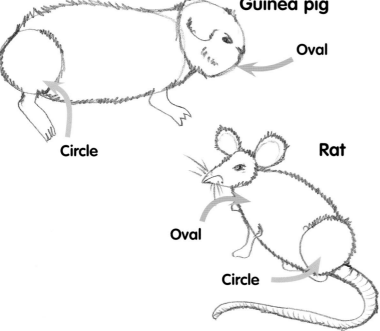

Rat
Oval
Circle

Top tips

• Lines and dots can be smudged with your finger to make a cat's fur look soft.

• Try erasing small areas of shading with an eraser to make highlights.

Fish, reptiles, and birds

You can draw fish, reptiles, and birds in the same way as cats and dogs, using simple shapes.

Top tip
Birds are the easiest pets to draw—all you need is a circle for the head, an oval body, and a long, pointed tail.

Bird

1 Draw a circle and an oval.
2 Add the wing and tail shapes.
3 Add the eye, beak, and feet.

Fish

1 Draw an oval head.
2 Draw two bulging eyes on both sides, and a curved mouth.
3 Add the tail and fins.

Snake

1 Start with a simple curved line.
2 Draw the rest of the body.
3 Add the snake's eye, tongue, and markings.

Scales and feathers

Scales can be drawn neatly, in rows. Notice how scales often overlap each other. You can add some shading, too.

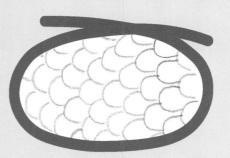

Lizard

1 Draw two ovals and a tail.
2 Add the legs.
3 Draw patterns on the lizard's body. Don't forget its tongue!

Use long, straight lines to draw large feathers on a bird's wings and tail.

Use short, curved lines to draw short, soft feathers on a bird's head and chest.

Turtle

1 Draw half an oval for the shell and the head.
2 Add the legs.
3 Draw markings on the shell and legs.

Click for Art!

To see children's drawings of birds and snakes, go to **www.junglephotos.com**. Enter the search term "children's artwork" and then follow the link.

Cities

City streets are full of exciting shapes. Follow the steps below to make your own city scene.

Top tip
The next time you visit a big city, look carefully at the buildings. What do you notice about the shapes of doors, windows, and roofs?

1 Lightly sketch the outline of different buildings across the bottom of the paper.

2 Draw taller buildings behind. Use a ruler to keep your lines straight.

City at night

This picture of a city at night has been drawn with bright red, yellow, white, and blue crayons on black paper.

Curved sides of buildings make the picture look more exciting.

Use tiny colored dashes for lit-up windows.

3 Sketch in building details such as doors and windows. Make details smaller in the **background**, so some buildings look farther away.

4 Go over the outlines of your buildings in wax crayons or pastels. Use a different color for each building.

5 Color in the rest of your picture using strong, bright colors. Paint a blue sky behind your city, or cut out a row of buildings and glue it to a sheet of colored paper.

Click for Art!

To see Robert Delaunay's "The Red Tower," go to **www.artchive.com/artchive/D/delaunay/red_tower.jpg.html**.

Countryside

In the country, shapes are rounded and softer than in the city. Follow the steps to draw a scene with different tree shapes and rounded hills.

You will need:
- Large sheet of sketch paper
- Colored chalks, pastels, or crayons

1 Lightly sketch the shapes of the trees (see "Drawing trees" on page 19 for tips).

2 Draw the rounded hills. Make them smaller as they get farther away.

3 Draw the shapes of smaller trees in the distance.

4 Color in the drawing with chalks, pastels, or crayons.

Drawing trees

1 Lightly sketch the trunk and outline of the tree.

2 Draw the main branches. Make each branch thick near the trunk and thinner at the end.

3 Use different shades of green for the leaves. Make the top leaves pale and the lower leaves darker, where it is more shady.

Click for Art!

To see a landscape by Monet, go to **www.ibiblio.org/ wm/paint/auth/monet** and click on "First Impressionist paintings."

19

Still life

A still life is a drawing or painting of something that does not move, such as flowers in a vase or a bowl of fruit.

1 Take time arranging the fruit in a bowl or on a tabletop until you are happy with the way it looks.

2 Lightly sketch the outline of the bowl first, then draw the fruit. Start with the pieces at the front of the bowl.

You will need:
- Something to draw, such as a bowl of fruit or a flower
- Colored pencils, chalks, crayons, or pastels

Tiny lines give the orange peel a rough texture.

Shading makes the fruit look rounded and three-dimensional.

  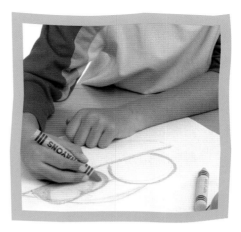

3 Draw the pieces of fruit at the back. Only draw the parts of the fruit you can see.

4 Go over your outlines in crayon, chalk, or pastel.

5 Color in or shade your picture.

Top tip

Before you start, look carefully at what you are going to draw. It sounds obvious, but many people who try to draw don't do that!

A colorful still life of flowers in a vase

Click for Art!

To see still-life paintings by Paul Cézanne, go to **www.ibiblio.org/wm/paint/auth/cezanne/sl**.

Self-portrait

One of the best ways to learn how to sketch people's faces is to draw pictures of yourself. First sketch a quick self-portrait from memory on scrap paper.

Perfect portraits

Is your face round, oval, heart-shaped, square, or long? If you can't tell, use a soft pencil or crayon and trace the shape of your face on a mirror—then you can look at the outline and tell what shape it is.

Before you start your self-portrait, think about your features. What shape are your eyes? Are your lips thin or full? Is your nose long or short?

Follow the steps on page 23. Look carefully at your reflection and draw a picture of your face. Think about the **shading** and **texture**.

Compare it with the first sketch you did—you'll be amazed how much better your new drawing is!

Start by looking carefully at yourself in the mirror. Think about where your ears are in relation to your eyes and nose.

Follow these steps to help you get all your features in the right place:

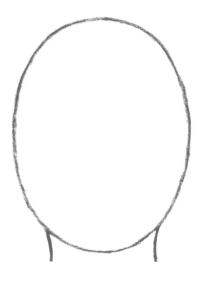

1 Use a soft pencil to sketch a faint egg shape for the **outline** of your face.

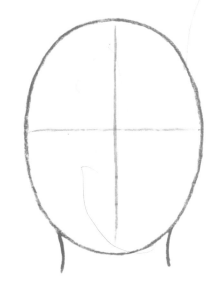

2 Draw a line down the middle of the face, and another one just above the center from side to side.

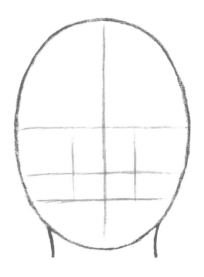

3 Now divide the lower half into two. Then draw three more lines: one across and two up and down, as shown.

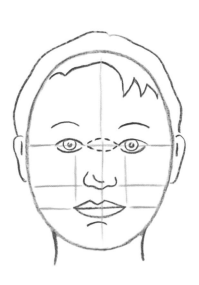

4 Use the lines as a guide to sketch in your eyes. Leave one eye width between them. Draw your mouth: start with the line between the lips, then add the outline of the upper and lower lips. Draw in the tip of your nose, but not the sides.

5 Add your ears, hair, eyelashes, eyebrows, chin, and other details. Now you can add shading and color with colored pencils.

Drawing faces

When you feel confident about drawing yourself, try drawing other people. Faces come in all shapes and sizes, and everyone's features are different. You can build up hundreds of different faces by making an "identikit set."

Identikit set

1 Draw four or five different face shapes, and divide them into sections.

2 Now cut lots of strips of paper, each the same width as the sections in the face.

3 Draw different-shaped eyes on some of the strips, noses on others, and mouths on the rest, all with different expressions.

4 Now mix and match the features on the different faces. You can cut out hairlines, moustaches, and glasses, too.

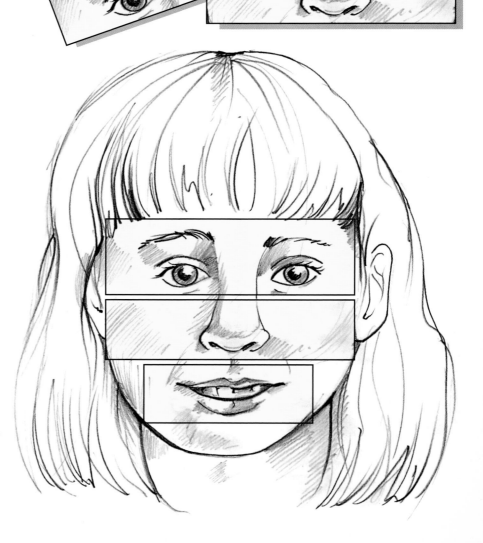

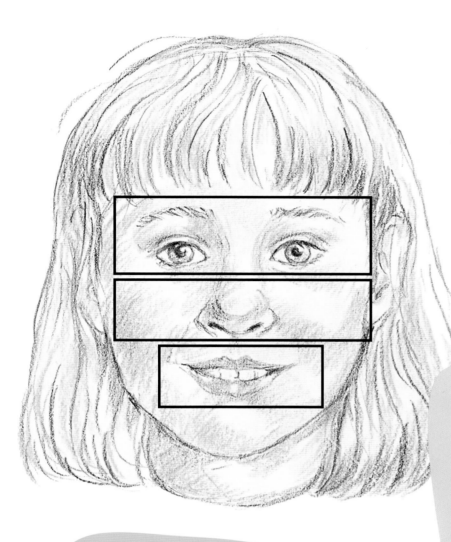

5 When you've created a face you like, trace or copy the **outline** and features onto another piece of paper. Use colored pencils to turn it into a finished drawing.

Art file

People don't smile all the time! Collect photos and newspaper cuttings of faces with different expressions, and practice drawing them.

Egg-heads

It's not quite as easy to draw people's faces from the side, or from above or below! A hard-boiled egg can be a very useful part of your art kit.

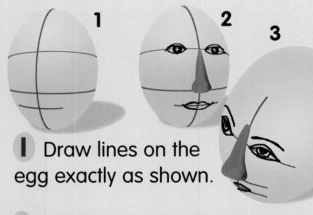

1 Draw lines on the egg exactly as shown.

2 Draw in the features. Stick a blob of clay on for the nose.

3 Using your egg-head as a model, practice drawing faces from different angles.

People in poses

When you're drawing a figure, think of the head as an egg, and the arms and legs as sausages or tubes. Use this technique to draw people in different poses.

1 Start with the head at the top of your paper. Draw an egg shape.

2 Add a short tube for the neck. It should be almost as wide as the head.

3 Now draw an egg shape for the top of the body.

4 Draw the arms as if they were two sausage shapes joined in the middle.

5 Draw the rest of the body using egg shapes and circles.

6 Draw the legs in the same way as the arms, but make them wider at the top.

7 Finally, add simple hand and feet shapes and draw the final outline to your figure.

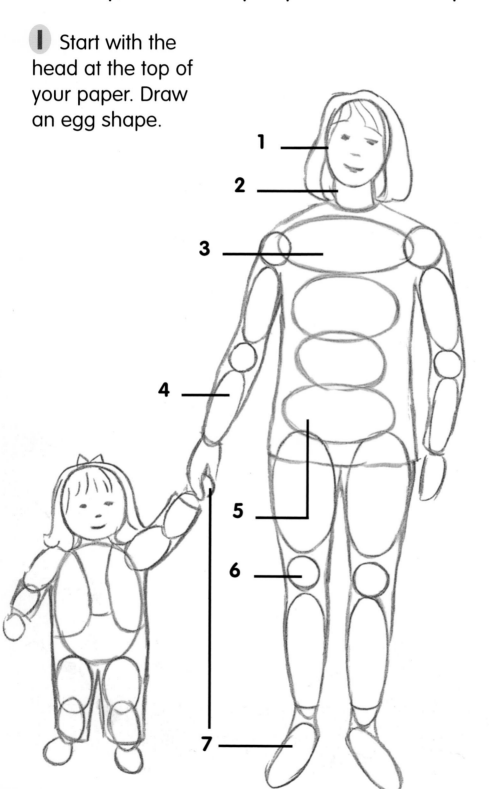

Now draw your sausage and egg figures sitting, lying, or crawling. Look at people in different poses or from different angles to get some ideas.

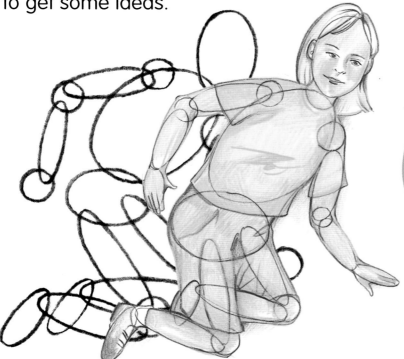

Try this

If you draw these shapes roughly at first, you can add the details later. Sketch lightly with a soft pencil. Erase the original lines when your drawing is complete.

Make a poster

Find some photos of your favorite sports, movie, or music star, and draw him or her by building up from simple shapes.

Use different pens, pencils, and crayons for your picture. What different effects can you create? Remember to use **shading** for the dark areas and leave **highlights** for the light areas.

SOCCER

27

Drawing a view

When it comes to drawing a view, how do you decide which parts to put in, and which to leave out? Making a viewfinder can help you decide.

Make a viewfinder

A viewfinder is a piece of cardboard with a hole in the middle. Make it out of two L-shaped pieces of cardboard, and you can adjust the shape to make a square or a rectangle.

1 Cut an L-shape out of cardboard. Trace around it to make an identical shape, and cut this one out, too.

2 Use paper clips to hold the pieces together and make a rectangle.

1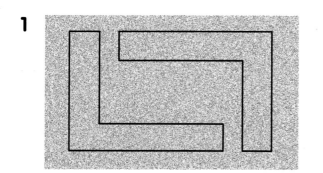

2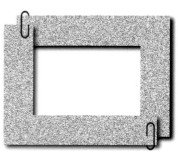

Top tip

Silver or white pencils look good on black **construction paper**. Use black pens or felt-tips to draw **silhouettes**—such as a winter **landscape** or a sunset. Silhouettes are solid dark **outlines** on a lighter **background**. They look good against soft white tissue paper or silver backgrounds.

1

Using the viewfinder

1 Hold the viewfinder in front of you. Look through the hole in the middle as if it were a camera lens. Move it around until you find the right view. What happens when you look at the same view **horizontally** and **vertically**?

2 When you have chosen your view, quickly sketch the main parts of the picture with a soft pencil (you can erase it later) using one hand. This is your rough outline for the finished picture to indicate large areas such as grass, sky, or water. Sketch in the positions of any buildings or trees.

3 When you have done the outlines, put the viewfinder away and finish the picture, putting in the details and using colored pencils, chalks, or pastels.

2

3

29

Looking at trees

As with all your drawings, it is important to look carefully at a tree before you try to draw it. Notice how the branches grow from one another, rather than all coming straight from the trunk.

There are a huge variety of tree shapes.

Some trees have long branches that reach out to the side.

Some trees are very tall and thin.

Up close

Tree bark varies a lot, too. Rubbings are a great way to collect different types of bark for reference. Put a piece of white paper over a section of the trunk and rub the surface with a soft pencil or crayon.

It can help to sketch the overall shape of a tree before you draw in the details. Try filling the whole piece of paper with your tree shape to make it really dramatic.

1 Lightly sketch in the trunk and the overall **outline** of the tree.

2 Draw the main branches, making them thinner at the ends.

3 Add fine lines for the smaller twigs, right up to the edge of the outline.

 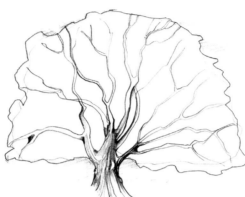 

This is how the tree looks in winter, but deciduous trees change throughout the year. Leaves appear, change color, and fall; buds can be followed by blossoms, and then berries.

Soft pencils or charcoal are ideal for drawing wintry trees. For a dramatic effect, use white chalk on black paper. Just color the spaces around the tree and in between the branches to make dramatic **silhouettes**.

 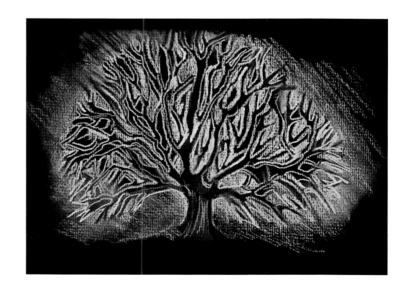

Cityscapes

A cityscape is a view of a city. Don't worry if you think buildings are too complicated to draw—the trick is to look at everything carefully and to build up the picture from patterns and shapes.

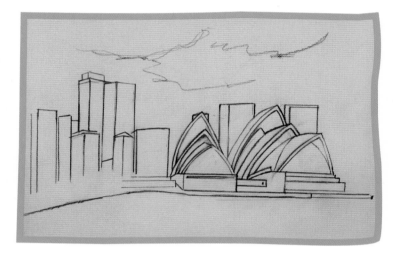

1 Decide what you are going to put into your picture. Are there any interesting buildings in your area? Use your viewfinder to help you decide which is the best view. You could use a scene from a postcard or from a book.

2 First, draw the **outlines** on a wide piece of paper. Look carefully at the buildings—are they wider than they are tall? Do the roofs slope steeply or are they shallow?

3 When you have done the outlines, sketch in the doors and windows. Check how big they are compared to the rest of the building.

4 Add the other details, such as chimneys, turrets, porches, steps, stones, wood, and brick patterns. Finish by adding color, using white to create **highlights** for bright spots.

Build your own

To make a building look three-dimensional, you need to draw its side view in addition to its front.

1 Draw the front of the building.

2 Draw in the sides to make a **cube**.

3 Add a roof, door, and windows.

4 Shade the side of the house lightly—you could add a shadow to make it look realistic.

1

2

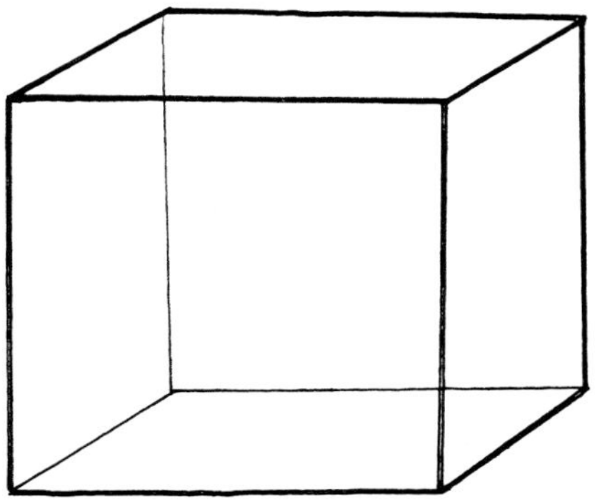

3

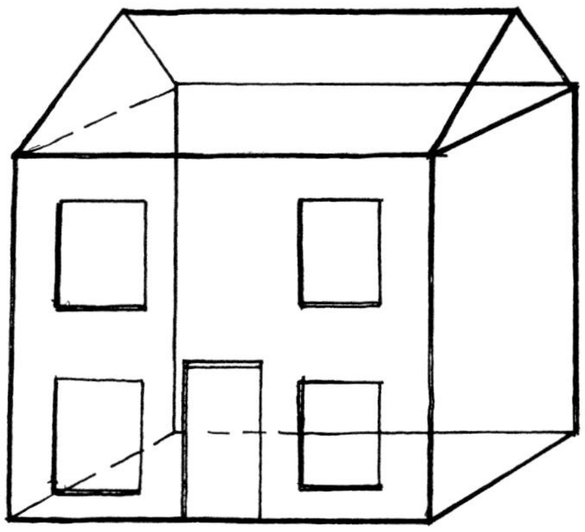

4

Using a grid

Drawing is about looking and copying exactly what you see. Sometimes our mind tricks us and we draw what we expect to see, not what is actually in front of us. Using a grid can help you get the **proportions** just right and can also help you make your pictures larger or smaller.

1 Take a photo or magazine cutting, and trace the **outline** of the picture you want to copy onto tracing paper. Now divide your tracing into equal squares, using a ruler to help you.

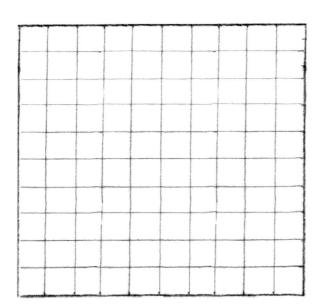

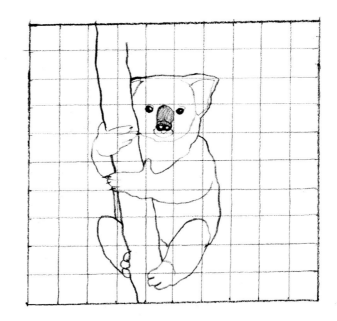

2 On a sheet of paper, make the same number of squares using a soft pencil. You can make the squares the same size as the ones on the tracing paper, or they can be smaller or bigger.

3 Copy the main outlines of the picture into each square one by one. Concentrate on each square one at a time, rather than looking at the whole picture.

Upside-down drawing

Choose a picture from a magazine that you'd like to draw, and draw a grid over it. Make a separate grid on a sheet of white paper. Turn the original picture upside down. Now copy each square, including all the **shading**. Your finished picture will be much more accurate, because you are just copying areas of color and shade, rather than trying to draw the details.

Using a piece of wallpaper lining, make a big poster of an animal for your wall. Use the grid technique with chalks or charcoals to fill in large areas quickly.

4 When the main outline is complete, erase the guidelines and fill in the smaller details, using the photo as a guide.

Make a dragon head

Dragons appear in a lot of Viking art because they are fierce, wild, and mysterious— just like famous Viking heroes.

You will need:
- Tracing paper
- Pencil
- Ruler
- Cardboard
- Black and white paint
- Paintbrushes
- Craft knife

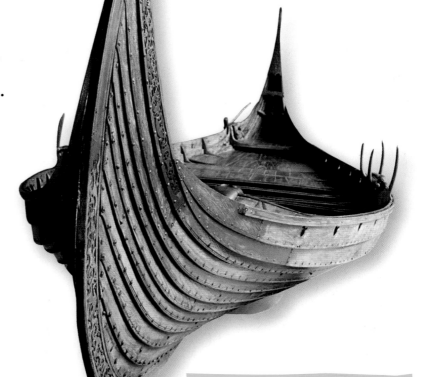

This 70-foot-long wooden ship has a snake-shaped prow. It was made in Norway more than 1,000 years ago.

A snarling beast, carved in wood; it was found in the ship above. Similar carvings were used on the prows of Viking warships.

1 Draw a grid of 1-inch squares onto tracing paper. Put the grid over the dragon at left and draw around it.

2 On a cardboard sheet, draw a large grid of 4-inch squares. Both grids need the same number of squares.

3 Copy the contents of each square on the tracing paper grid into the matching square on the big grid.

4 Mix white and black paint to make gray. Paint your dragon head and leave it to dry completely.

5 Ask an adult to cut out your dragon head. Draw on the dragon's features with black paint.

Did you know?
In winter, when rivers, lakes, and bogs were frozen, Vikings traveled on sleds, skates, and skis.

Cartoon tips and hints

Anyone can draw cartoons—the more you practice, the better you'll become! Start with a person, an animal, or an object—or use your imagination to create a fantasy character or monster.

What is a cartoon?

What makes cartoons different from other drawings? Think about your favorite cartoon character from movies, television, comic strips, or picture books.

The Simpsons, **created by Matt Groening, is popular all over the world.**

Animal magic

Look carefully at different animals and make sketches of them. Look at books, magazines, or the Internet. You could also watch wildlife programs on television or use a microscope to look at tiny insects.

People pictures

Look carefully at your family, friends, or favorite celebrities. Everyone has a unique **feature** that would make a great cartoon. Collect photos of people in different outfits, positions, and poses. Look at them for ideas when you draw your cartoons.

Cool cartoons

You can get different effects depending on which tools you use. Use a black pen or felt-tip to **outline** and **shade** your cartoons. Felt-tips create bold outlines and flat color. Colored inks give a softer effect. Combine a black ink outline with pencils, colored ink, or **watercolors**.

Cartoon figures

The easiest way to draw a cartoon figure is to sketch a simple **outline** first, and then add the details. You can start by drawing stick figures or round people. Begin by trying the cartoon figure below.

Stick figures

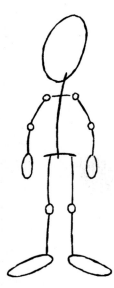

1 Draw a stick figure with oval head, hands, and feet. Put small circles at the joints.

2 Build up the figure by adding more ovals for the body, such as for the shoulders and hips.

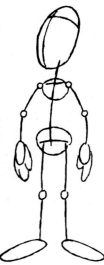

3 Draw in the basic **features** of the face.

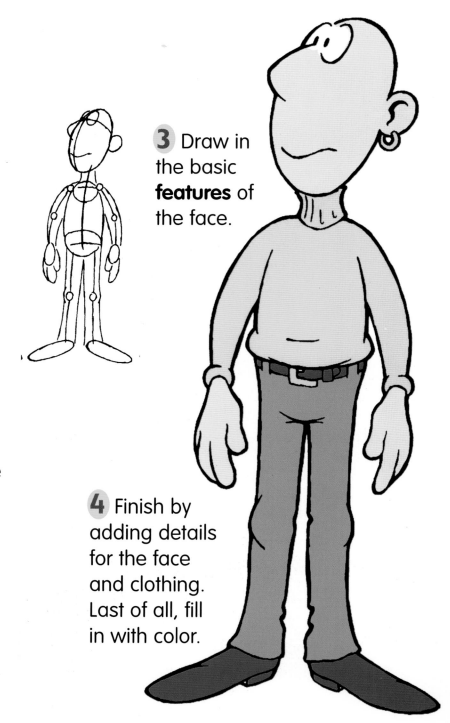

4 Finish by adding details for the face and clothing. Last of all, fill in with color.

Top tip

You can use circles and ovals to make cartoon figures: stretched ovals make tall, skinny cartoons; circles make plump people. Mix the two to create fat people with spindly legs.

Big and little

To draw cartoons of people you know, look at them carefully. Are they tall or short? Do they have a lot of hair? Now exaggerate their most outstanding feature. Practice drawing from photographs.

1 Draw the outline of your figure using circles or ovals.

2 Now add details to make them funny, such as hair, shoes, and clothes.

Faces and features

Faces and **expressions** are important in cartoons. Start at the top. First draw the head shapes, then add the different features. You can easily make your cartoon character look ahead or sideways.

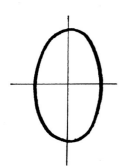

Head-on!

1 Draw an oval. Divide it into quarters.

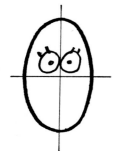

2 Put in the eyes just above the center.

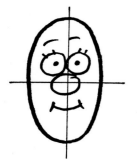

3 Add the nose on the center line. Add the mouth halfway down.

4 Add hair, eyebrows, and eyelashes. Make your faces happy, sad, or scared.

Top tip

Try different face shapes: long and thin, short and fat! Fat heads have no neck. Thin heads look skinnier on a long, thin neck.

Hair can make a big difference to your characters. Different styles can make characters look messy or glamorous, young or old.

If you are making someone you know into a cartoon, look at them carefully. What do you notice most about them? Do they have a long chin? A wide face? Ears that stick out? A big nose? Glasses? These are the features you can exaggerate to make a great cartoon.

Remember glasses and jewelry. Details bring cartoons to life.

Top tip

Look at your reflection in the back of a serving spoon. With your face in the light against a dark background, draw what you see. Your face will be stretched and distorted. Draw this for an instant cartoon effect.

On the move

Now that you've created your cartoon characters, you need to make them move. Follow these hints and tips to make them run, jump, or even fly.

Head-on!

1 Begin with a simple figure.

2 Add ovals and circles.

3 Now add clothes, color, and facial **expressions**.

Jumping

Running

Movement lines help to show which way something is moving—and how fast.

Top tip
Movement lines also add extra action to your cartoon—just look at the pictures below. Adding double movement lines behind these figures makes them look more active.

Cartoon creatures

Before you start drawing cartoon animals, practice sketching real ones. Then try turning your sketches into cartoons.

Drawing animals

Notice the **features** and personalities of a variety of animals. A dog's ears can be droopy or perky, depending on whether it is happy or sad.

Kooky animals

You can make any kind of animal from simple shapes:

1   2   3   4

Animal shapes

1

1 Draw an **outline** of the head and body, using circles and ovals. Add the legs, feet, and tail.

2

2 Erase the guidelines that you don't want in the final picture.

3

3 Use colored pencils or pens to finish the drawing.

When you are confident about drawing animals, try stretching the body and limbs to make them taller and skinnier, or squash them for rounder, fatter, more comical cartoon creatures.

Create a new animal star
Some animals have been turned into cartoons many times before—especially bears and cats! Try to think of something more unusual and see what you can do with it. Will it be fierce or friendly? Smart or stupid? Fast or slow?

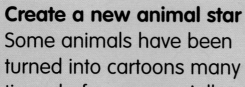

47

It's alive!

Cartoons can make anything come to life. Look around your bedroom for inspiration— or your backyard or classroom. You can make your whole street into cartoon characters. The windows can be the eyes of the houses and the doors can be mouths.

Kitchen cartoons

Choose an object and get to know it well. Draw it so often, and from so many different angles, that it becomes as familiar as a friend.

Give it a name and turn its parts into human features: a spout or handle can become a nose, for example.

Motor mouths

Give bikes, cars, scooters, skateboards, boats, trains, and buses funny faces to bring them to life. Try to make the shapes match the expressions—for example, a car can be round, smiley, and friendly or long, mean, and aggressive, with a long radiator that looks like a mouthful of flashing teeth, and evil eyes instead of headlights.

Scary monsters

People, animals, buildings, or houses can make scary cartoons—and that's even before you start drawing the real monsters, such as vampires, werewolves, and ghosts!

Everyone will recognize a vampire. How about coming up with your own monsters?

Wicked witches are usually ugly and have pointed noses, long chins, and warts on their faces.

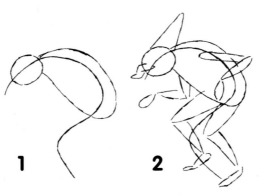

1

2

3

You can make ghosts as black **silhouettes**, or as white, cloudy shapes with a soft, black **outline** in the shape of a whirlwind.

Monster tip
Try mixing parts of different animals into a new fantasy friend or fiend.

A question of size
Even tiny creatures can become terrifying if they grow to a huge size.

Mythical monsters
Myths and legends are full of strange and scary creatures, such as dragons, werewolves, and devils. Choose a mythical monster and turn it into a cartoon. Will yours be scary, friendly, or funny?

Set the scene

After you've created a group of cartoon characters, it's fun to put them in different **backgrounds**. Use real-life situations or invent a fantasy world—your background can be more interesting than a blank piece of paper.

Top tip

Always start by sketching your cartoon character in soft pencil first, and then add the background. Add **foreground** details last. When you are happy with the finished result, color it in and go over the **outlines** with a thick black pen.

Where to get ideas

Look at travel magazines, photos, and books, or around your house, street, or school. Which of these scenes suits your cartoon characters? Draw some simple backgrounds—choose a few details that show where the location is meant to be.

Placing your character

Your character should appear to be part of the scene, not just stuck on top of it. Make sure that there is some detail in front of it as well as behind it.

Night or day?

Nighttime backgrounds are great for a spooky atmosphere. Draw your character and buildings in black **silhouette**.

In the mood

Different skies set the mood, too. It's easy to fill the sky with snow or rain.

Comic capers

Now that you've learned how to draw amazing cartoon figures, you can put them in your own comic story. First, take a look at some of your favorite comics. You'll see that the pages are split into **frames** of different sizes and shapes.

Frames don't have to be square! Try circles, ovals, and ones with jagged edges. You can draw the frames by hand so that they are not all straight lines, or draw them neatly with a ruler. Comic strips look more exciting if parts of the picture break out of the frame edges.

POW!

Storylines

Your characters can "talk" in speech and thought bubbles. If you need extra information, and have enough space, you can put words in boxes at the top or bottom of the picture. Speech bubbles are usually oval. Bubbles that look like clouds are used to show a character's thoughts. Jagged bubbles are for angry people, and shivery bubbles can be used for a character who is scared.

Exclamation marks!

These punctuation marks are used a lot in comics! To show people shouting, use a thick black marker.

Bubble tip

Speech and thought bubbles usually go in the top third of the picture, so draw your sketch in the bottom two-thirds.

Make a comic

Now that you've seen how it's done, try creating a comic strip with your own cast of funny, scary, or silly characters. You can even make a whole comic book from a collection of strips.

YOUR CARTOON CHARACTER CAN DO ANYTHING!

Lights, camera, action!

Making a comic strip is like making a movie: you need a story, a main character, a few minor characters, and a series of **backgrounds**. Start by thinking of a short, simple story with a beginning, a middle, and an end. Look through some joke books for a funny ending.

Stars of the show

What will your main character look like? Decide what sort of personality they have and think of a name. Try drawing them from lots of different angles to get them right. You also need friends and enemies for the main character to talk to. Try not to have more than three characters—otherwise readers may get confused.

Storyboarding

You're ready to make a storyboard. This is a rough sketch of each frame; it doesn't have to be perfect. Try to vary the pictures. Sometimes characters can be in the distance; other times you can show a close-up of their face and **expression**.

Comic frames

When you are happy with your storyboard, turn it into a finished comic strip. Draw each box neatly, with a ruler and pencil. Make sure you draw the frames big enough to fit in all the details you want.

Finishing off

Copy your drawings from the storyboard and turn them into finished cartoons. First, draw the **outlines** in pencil.

Go over the outlines with black marker or a felt-tip. Color in the pictures with paint or felt-tips. Your comic is complete!

Painting kit

You only need brushes and a paint set to create great pictures, but with a few extra materials you will also be able to experiment with exciting effects.

Top tip
Collect old jam jars to hold water to wash your brushes in.

Pencils

Pencils

Soft-lead pencils (such as 9B) are useful for sketching the outlines of your pictures before adding paint. Use colored pencils to add details.

Basic equipment
- Paper and poster paper
- Poster and **acrylic** paints
- **Watercolors**
- Pencils and paintbrushes
- Safety scissors
- White school glue
You will also need some extra items, which are listed separately for each project.

Brushes

Different brushes give different results. You need a fine, pointed one for details, one of medium thickness, and a really thick one for large areas. Nylon bristles are best for thin paint, and hogs' hair brushes are better for thick paint. Use an old toothbrush for spattering, and sponges and rags for dabbing.

Palettes and pots

You can buy artists' **palettes** for mixing colors—but an old plastic tray, an old plate, or piece of smooth wood are just as good. Use jars full of water to clean your brushes.

Brushes

Palette

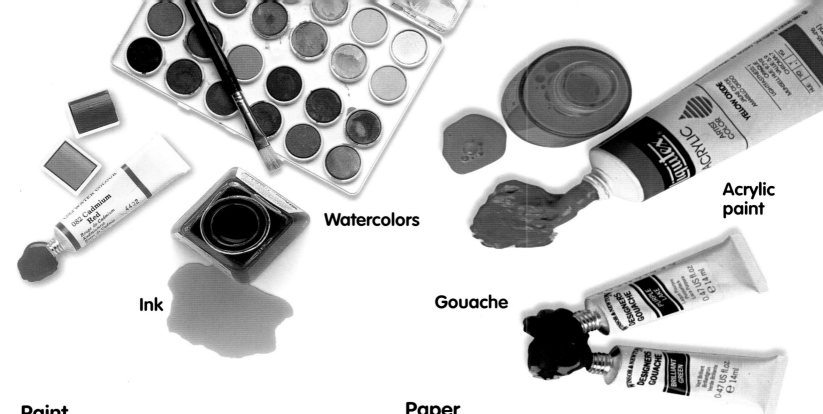

Watercolors

Ink

Acrylic paint

Gouache

Paint

Poster paints are ideal for big, bold paintings, or to mix with other things to create texture. Use them straight from the container or thin them down with water. **Watercolors** are delicate colors that make great landscapes. They come in tubes or blocks, are easy to carry, and are handy for color sketches. Gouache paints produce strong, vibrant colors that work well on colored papers.

Paper

It's important to use good paper. Smooth **sketch paper** is best, as the paint doesn't sink into the surface. Rough construction paper can be interesting. Watercolor paper is thick, so it doesn't wrinkle when it gets wet.

Art paper

Poster paints

Printing kit

This section will show you how to make fantastic prints from cardboard, sponges, leaves—even food. You can find almost everything you need around the house.

Basic equipment

- Paper and cardboard
- Poster/**acrylic** paints
- Pencils and paintbrushes
- Safety scissors
- White school glue
- Ruler

You will also need the extra items listed separately for each project.

Paper and cardboard

You can make prints on white or colored paper, card stock, posterboard, or cardboard.

Printing blocks

You can make printing blocks from craft foam, sponges, or cardboard.

Paints for printing

The best paints to use are poster paints or acrylic paints. Use fabric paints for printing on cloth.

Don't forget to spread some newspaper to work on, and to wear an apron to keep your clothes clean.

Take care!

Some of the projects involve cutting, ironing, and photocopying. Always ask an adult for help where you see this sign.

Craft supplies

Keep a big box full of things you can use to make prints. Look for items with interesting **textures** or shapes. For example:

★ The end of heavyweight corrugated cardboard
★ Old sponge or cork
★ Piece of yarn
★ Bubble wrap
★ Toy building bricks
★ Feather

Brushes and paint dishes

You will need paintbrushes of different sizes and some old dishes for mixing your paints.

A printing roller is also useful for spreading paint evenly on a flat surface.

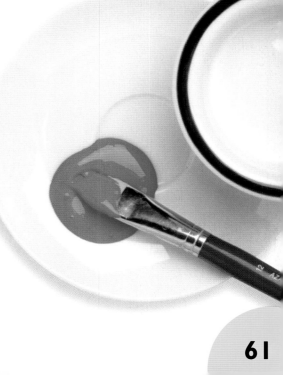

Splitter-splatter!

Make a lively painting by spattering paint onto paper with a brush or toothbrush.

You will need:
• Old toothbrush

1 Draw fish and starfish outlines on a sheet of paper. Turn the paper over and place it facedown on some newspaper.

2 Dip a toothbrush in yellow paint, then drag your finger over the bristles to spatter the paint on the paper. Try flicking yellow and orange paint with ordinary brushes, too.

3 Now flick blue and green paint onto a second sheet of paper. Use different shades of blue and green to make a speckled sea background.

Top tip
Paint spattering is messy! Wear an apron to protect your clothes, and spread out plenty of newspaper to work on.

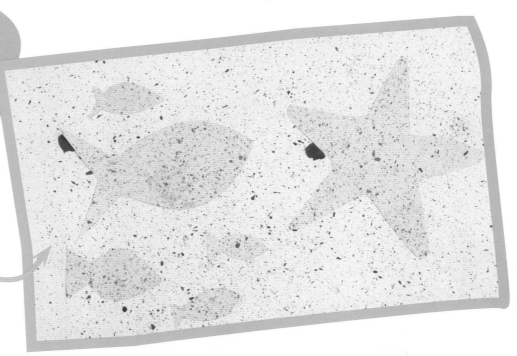

Follow the steps above to create this speckled underwater scene.

Click for Art!

To see "drip paintings" by the American artist Jackson Pollock, go to **http://www.artlex.com** and search for "action painting."

4 When the paint is dry, turn the paper over and cut out the fish and starfish with safety scissors. Arrange them on your sea background and glue them down.

Copy these shapes onto poster paper to create the desert landscape above.

Desert landscape

1 Make cardboard **stencils** using the shapes below.

2 Arrange the stencils on a sheet of thick white paper. Use a small dab of glue to hold them in place.

3 Spatter yellow paint over the bottom part of the paper for the sand. Spatter blue paint above for the sky.

4 When the paint is dry, remove the cardboard stencils.

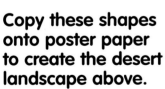

Straw paintings

Blowing paint through a straw makes the paint wander in wiggly lines and creates wonderful and unusual shapes.

Top tip
To mix colors, add a second color when the first is still wet. If you do not want your colors to mix, wait until the first color is dry before you add another.

You will need:
• Plastic drinking straw

1 Add water to some poster or acrylic paint to make the paint runny.

2 Drip a large blob of paint onto your paper with a brush.

3 Blow gently at the paint through the straw. The paint will spread across the paper in wiggly lines.

4 Add different colors one by one. (See "Top tip" on page 64 for hints on color mixing.)

Sometimes a straw painting may start to look like something recognizable— such as a fluffy chick, a flower, a person's hair, or an insect.

This chick's legs, eyes, and beak were added with pencil and orange crayon.

5 Add details with a crayon or brush to complete your painting.

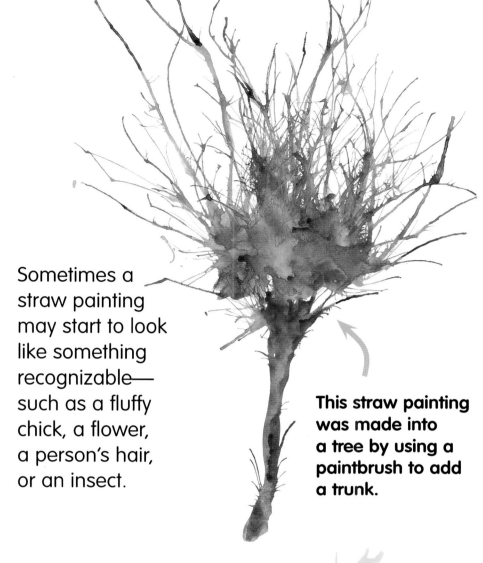

This straw painting was made into a tree by using a paintbrush to add a trunk.

Click for Art!

To explore paintings by Jackson Pollock, Mark Rothko, and Robert Rauschenberg, go to **www.sfmoma.org/ anderson.** Click on "Start Program" and then "Explore 15 works."

Dotty paintings

You will need:
• Paintbrush with a fine tip

To blend colors, try using a pattern of different-colored dots and dashes.

Mixing colors

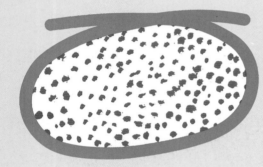

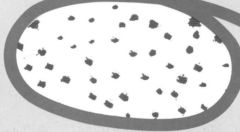

1 Before you begin your picture, practice making lots of tiny dots next to each other with the tip of your brush. Try one color first, such as red.

2 Now make some more red dots on a clean sheet of paper. This time, space the dots out a little.

3 When the red paint is dry, add yellow dots in between. Stand back. What color do the red and yellow dots look like from a distance?

4 Now try making dots and dashes with different colors and different-sized brushes.

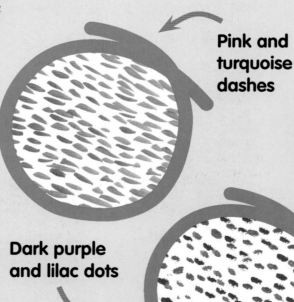

Pink and turquoise dashes

Dark purple and lilac dots

Blue and red blobs

Frog on a lily pad

Yellow dots highlight the frog's back

Top tip
Make darker dots and place them closer together to add detail and shading.

1 Plan your painting in your sketchbook or on a piece of scratch paper.

2 Lightly sketch the outline of your painting on a sheet of white paper.

3 Color each part of the picture with tiny dots of color. This dotty painting has dark green for the lily pads, pale green for the frog, and yellow and dark green dots for the frog's markings.

Click for Art!
To learn how the French painter Georges Seurat made paintings out of tiny dots, go to **www.metmuseum.org/Works_of_Art** and search for "Circus Sideshow."

67

Wax paintings

Use paint and wax crayons to make wax-**resist** paintings. The wax resists the paint, so the color of the crayons shows through.

1 Cover the bottom of your paper with a white crayon for snow.

You will need:
- Thick paper or poster paper
- Wax crayons
- Blue watercolor or poster paint

2 Still using crayons, add a snowman in the middle. Give him an orange carrot nose, two eyes, a black hat, some buttons, and a striped scarf.

3 Add white crayon dots for falling snow.

4 Mix dark blue paint for the background. If you are using poster paint, add water to make it thinner.

scraper effects

1 With wax crayons, create patches of bright color on thick paper.

2 Paint three layers of black, dark blue, or purple acrylic paint over the crayon patches.

Top tip

If you are making a scraper picture, be sure to use thick paper or cardboard, as ordinary paper may tear.

3 When the paint is dry, scrape a picture into the paint with a knitting needle. The bright colors will show through.

5 Brush the blue paint over your drawing. The crayon marks will resist the paint, so your drawing stands out.

Lost in space!

To make this picture, draw the rocket, planets, and stars first using bright crayons. Then add black watercolor paint on top.

Water paintings

Enjoy experimenting with watercolor paints. They are great for seas and skies!

You will need:
- Watercolor paper
- Watercolor paints
- Wide paintbrush
- Thin, pointed paintbrush
- Sponge, tissue paper, or cotton balls

1 Using a paintbrush, spread clean water all over your sheet of watercolor paper.

2 Paint yellow stripes over the top half of your paper. Add orange stripes halfway down.

3 Paint the sea using shorter brushstrokes. Use orange, yellow, and blue. Let the colors run a little.

Top tip
To help the colors in the sea run together, drip a few drops of clean water over the paint.

4 While the paint is still wet, dab a cotton ball on the yellow sky so the patches look like pale clouds.

5 When the paint is dry, paint a black island and a palm tree. If you want, add a shark's fin pointing out of the water!

Watery skies

For cloudy skies, paint overlapping stripes of blue watercolor paint across your paper. Before the paint dries, dab it with a clean sponge. This will leave white patches that look like clouds.

These clouds were made by painting stripes of blue across wet paper, then dabbing the paint with scrunched-up tissue paper.

For a different effect, let the blue paint dry, then paint clouds in white watercolor paint.

Click for Art!

To see watercolors by the English artist J. M. W. Turner, go to **www.j-m-w-turner.co.uk.** Click on "Turner in Venice," scroll down, and then click on the small pictures.

From a distance

Ever since the first artist picked up a brush, people have tried to paint the world around them. This project will help you capture lots of different views in your paintings.

Paint a 3-D theater

This **3-D** theater is made up of cards, one behind the other, to make the scenery look convincing. Just as in a painting, you should make the front scenery strong using bold colors and the more distant background parts paler.

1

1 Cut two squares of cardboard, each 7 inches square. Use a ruler to divide them into ten ¾-inch lines.

3 Glue the accordion sides onto a cardboard base. Cut out five rectangles, each 7 x 9 inches. Paint one blue for the sky. Glue it to the sides to make the **backdrop**. Cut another rectangle into a frame shape and glue it to the front.

2 Fold along the lines to make two **accordion** shapes for the sides of your theater.

2

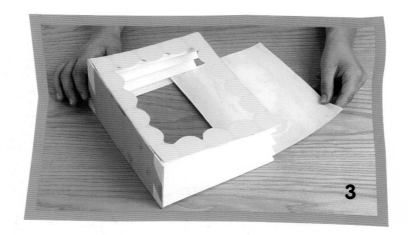

3

4 The three remaining rectangles are for your scenery. Draw a country scene on one softly in pencil, with a house at the top. The other two pieces should be rolling hedges. Draw these so that they are not as tall as the house scenery. The smaller scenes will slot in the front.

4

5 Now color the scenery. Remember to use soft, pale colors in the distance and strong, sharp details at the front. Finally, cut the pieces out, ready to slot into place in your 3-D theater.

5

Create different sets of scenery for your theater. How about a city at night?

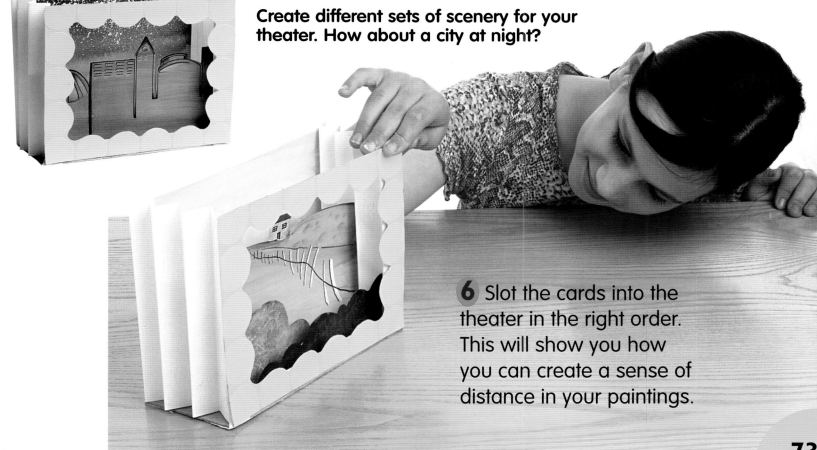

6 Slot the cards into the theater in the right order. This will show you how you can create a sense of distance in your paintings.

Paint a Viking stone

The Vikings painted stones to record their history and stories of gods and monsters. Make your own Viking stone in five easy steps.

You will need:
- Smooth stone
- Chalk or white pencil
- Acrylic paints
- Paintbrushes
- Gold metallic pen
- Acrylic varnish or glue mixture (3 parts white school glue, 1 part water)

Did you know?
These are all Viking words: both, drag, egg, fall, gale, knife, score, scold, ship, sling, slug, smile, want, whirl, whistle, window, and wing.

The Viking homelands in northern Europe were surrounded by stormy seas to the east, west, and south, and by Arctic ice to the north.

ICELAND
NORWAY
GREENLAND
SWEDEN
ATLANTIC OCEAN
DENMARK
RUSSIA
NEWFOUNDLAND
Normandy

This monster face with horns and a long beard was carved on a stone in Denmark.

1 Find a smooth stone in the yard or park. Wash it in soapy water, rinse, and leave it to dry.

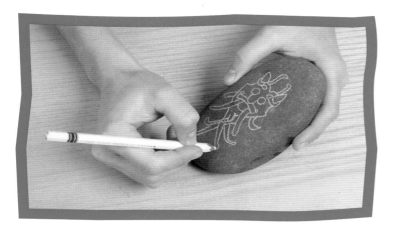

2 With a white pencil or chalk, carefully copy the picture on the opposite page onto your stone.

3 Paint the face blue, except for the eyes and mouth. Paint the mouth red and add a white dot on each side.

Use your stone as a paperweight or display it on a shelf.

4 Paint the eyes light blue. Once all the paint is dry, use a gold metallic pen to go over your lines.

5 Use a clean brush to add a coat of varnish or glue mixture. Leave to dry, then add another coat.

Montezuma's headdress

Aztec rulers wore splendid headdresses made of priceless feathers and gold. Now you can wear one, too!

Aztecs making a feather fan (left) and a feather headdress (right).

This headdress probably belonged to the great Aztec ruler Montezuma, who ruled in the 16th century.

You will need:

- Compass
- Card stock
- Pencil
- Ruler
- Scissors
- Paint
- Paintbrushes
- Gold glitter glue
- Green, blue, and turquoise paper
- Tape

1 Set your compass to 3 inches. Draw a semicircle and cut it out. Cut out a smaller one in the center.

2 Paint on stripes of blue, green, and brown for feathers. When dry, add dots of gold using glitter glue.

3 Make a feather template. Use it to draw and cut out 12 feathers from some blue and green paper.

4 Tape each of the feathers around the back of the mask. Try to alternate the colors.

Ask an adult or friend to help you tape the ends of the card strip together at the back. Add a centerpiece, as shown, if you like.

5 Cut out a card strip long enough to go around your head, with an overlap of 1 inch. Glue the headdress to the strip.

Did you know?

The Aztecs received brightly colored feathers from hunters who lived in the rain forests. The best feathers, from the blue-green quetzal bird, were more valuable than gold.

Abstract art

You don't have to make your paintings look realistic if you don't want to. Many famous artists painted what they saw using flat patterns, bright colors, and interesting shapes. This is called **abstract** art.

Different styles

Many artists moved away from realistic painting and developed styles of their own. Pablo Picasso often used a style called **Cubism**, where everything is made of blocks of color. Henri Matisse made collages with cutout shapes.

"L'Escargot" (The Snail) by Henri Matisse

Top tip
Henri Matisse often used torn and cut paper to make bold collage images. Try making a collage of your artwork, using pieces of colored paper instead of paint.

Make an abstract painting

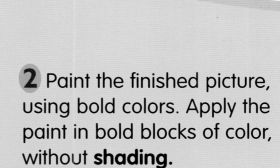

Decide what you are going to paint—for example, the view from your window, a scene from a postcard, a person, or an animal.

1 Lightly sketch the main parts of the picture with a pencil. Just draw the houses and trees as simple shapes. In this painting, the artist hasn't tried to put anything in the right place—he has just used them to make a pattern of shapes and colors.

2 Paint the finished picture, using bold colors. Apply the paint in bold blocks of color, without **shading.**

Painting patterns

Flowers, berries, and leaves make great patterns. Look for examples in your yard or local park. Look through magazines, wallpaper samples, and fabric scraps to see how artists use natural forms in their designs. You can also make your own nature patterns.

You will need:
- Pencil
- Thick paper
- Poster paints
- Scissors
- Glue
- Collection of leaves, petals, or twigs

Design your own wallpaper or material

1 Look through your collection of leaves, flowers, and plants and sketch some of your favorite shapes.

2 Make a pattern with the shapes—cut them up and arrange them on the page, then glue them in place.

3 For a repeat design, draw a grid with a pencil and ruler. This will help you keep the shapes straight, the same size, and in the right place. Your shapes can be realistic or imaginative.

4 Paint the pattern using poster paint. Which works best—two or three colors, or more? Why not try some different designs?

Top tip
English Victorian artists often used nature in their designs. William Morris used plants, flowers, and birds in wallpaper, tapestries, stained-glass windows, tiles, and **embroidery**.

Dragging and combing

Dragging and combing pictures and designs in thick, wet paint is a fun way to create images.

1 Cut comb shapes out of cardboard. Make some with thick teeth and some with small teeth.

2 Brush a thick coat of paint onto the paper in different colors. Divide the page into roughly equal bands of color.

3 While the paint is still wet, drag your card combs through the paint to make waves and lines. The colors will carry over into the other bands, and in some places you will see the paper beneath.

Scraper art

In addition to making patterns, you can use your scrapers to make a picture.

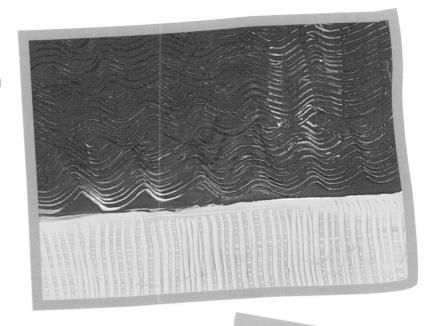

1 Paint a wide band of yellow across the bottom of the paper and fill in the rest of the page with blue paint. While the paint is still wet, use a cardboard comb to make swirly waves in the sea. Use a comb to make **horizontal** lines across the sand, then comb upward for a **checkered** effect.

2 On a separate piece of paper, use paint and combs to make sea animals and plants.

3 When these are dry, cut them out and glue them to the sea and sand background.

Add details like the eye on the fish using a felt-tip pen when your painting is dry.

Watercolor art

You can get some wonderful effects if you brush watery paint onto wet paper. The colors blend together, giving a very soft result.

You will need:
- Watercolor paint
- Wide, soft paintbrush
- Thick paper
- Glass jar for water

Two-color painting

Practice using two colors to make watery paintings.

1 Use a wide, soft paintbrush to wet the paper. Then paint a wide strip of yellow across the bottom half of the paper.

2 Before it dries, dip your brush in the second color. Brush this gently over the top so that the two colors merge softly. Work quickly before the paint dries!

Top tip

If you don't want your paintings to go crinkly when they dry, stretch the paper first. Dip the paper very quickly in water, and tape it to a board or piece of cardboard. Once dry, it is ready to use.

Paint a sunset

1 Brush water all over the paper with a wide, soft brush. Paint the background in yellow and, while the paint is wet, add some orange streaks.

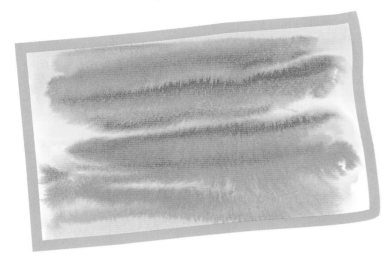

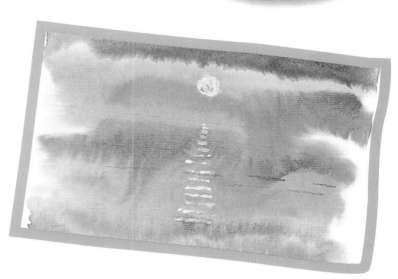

2 Now use some dark blue paint to add a band at the top of the image. Let this dry before using white paint to add the sun and its reflection in the water.

3 Use black paint to make the strip of land about three-quarters of the way up the picture. Add some ripples in light blue in the foreground.

4 When the paint is dry, use a small brush to add the boats with black paint. They appear as **silhouettes** in the sunset, with dark reflections in the water.

Spatter art

Some artists don't use brushes to paint objects, they just throw the paint onto their pictures! It is a great way of making a fun, lively image with lots of color.

Make your own messy masterpiece

1 Cover the floor with newspaper and wear an apron or artist's smock. Put your sheet of paper in the middle.

2 Flick runny paint onto the paper with brushes. Dip the toothbrush into paint, and run the cardboard over the bristles while you point it at the paper.

3 Add blobs, drizzles, and splats of different colors until you like the result. Leave some white background showing through.

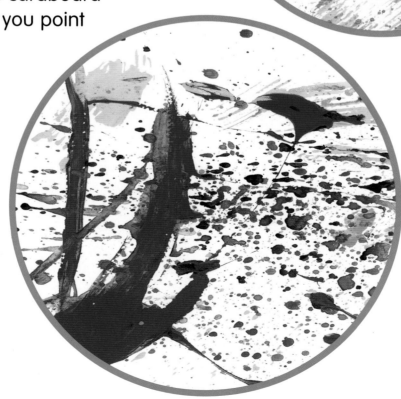

Spatter stencils

Spattering over a stencil makes a sharp image on a messy background.

1 Cut some shapes out of cardboard. Arrange them on a piece of paper.

2 Spatter the paint over the paper as before. Carefully lift up the shapes when you have finished.

Top tip
If you want to make one or more areas of your picture darker, dip a toothbrush in paint, hold it near the area you want to make darker, and keep flicking the paint at the paper using your thumb.

Going BIG!

Choose strong, simple images for a large painting or mural. The trick is to plan them first on a sheet of paper. Then it's easy to scale them up in size.

Using a grid to scale up

1 Sketch out your drawing or design on a standard sheet of paper. Paint in the colors you want to use.

2 When the paint has dried, draw a square using a ruler and pencil around your picture. Mark off 2-inch intervals on each side of the square. Join the marks to make a grid. Draw a grid over the picture. If the picture doesn't divide exactly into 2-inch squares, make the bottom rows slightly smaller.

Top tip

If you don't want to spoil your first painting, tape a piece of tracing paper over the top, and draw the grid on this.

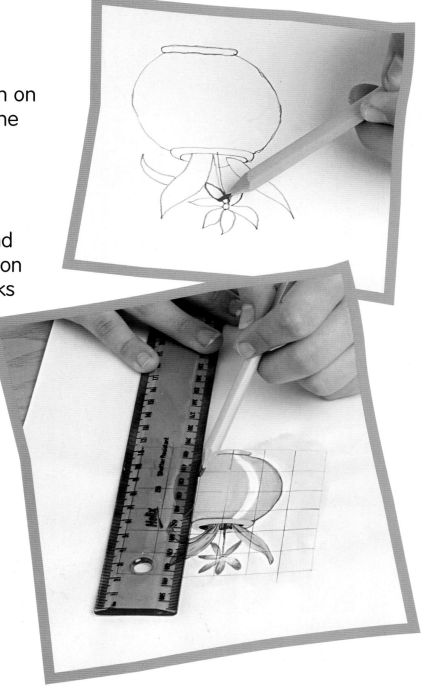

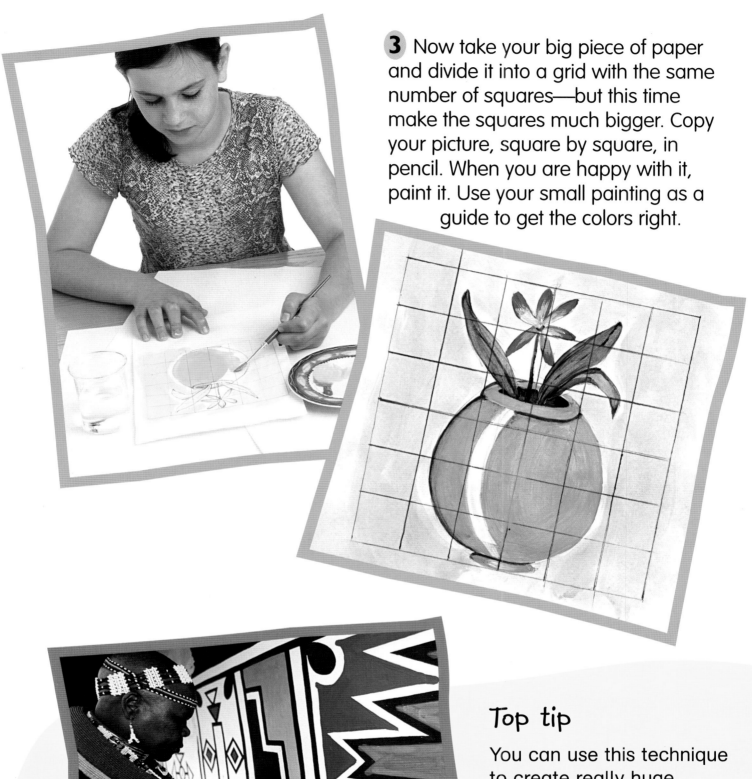

3 Now take your big piece of paper and divide it into a grid with the same number of squares—but this time make the squares much bigger. Copy your picture, square by square, in pencil. When you are happy with it, paint it. Use your small painting as a guide to get the colors right.

Top tip

You can use this technique to create really huge pictures. All over the world, people make large images to decorate the walls of their houses or streets. Try making a large image for your classroom wall.

Body prints

You can make fantastic prints with your hands or fingertips! Just follow these easy steps.

Top tip
Keep a bowl of soapy water and a towel handy. Clean your fingers before you dip them in a new color.

Butterfly frieze

1 Paint green grass and blue sky on a large sheet of paper and leave it to dry.

You will need:
• Large sheet of white paper
• A few sheets of white posterboard
• Felt-tip pen or pipe cleaners

2 Ask an adult to help you photocopy and cut out butterfly shapes like this from white posterboard.

Apple prints

1 Paint your palm with red paint and press it onto paper.

2 Make a brown stalk by printing with the side of a short piece of cardboard.

3 Press your thumb into green paint to print some leaves.

3 Dip your fingertips in paint and press them onto the cut-out butterfly shapes.

Use your fingertips to print these fun animals, then add details with a felt-tip pen.

4 Glue the shapes onto the **background**. Draw feelers with a felt-tip pen, or glue on pipe cleaners.

Click for Art!

To see ancient handprints on cave walls in Australia, go to **www.dvc.vic.gov.au/aav/heritage/mini-posters/14RockArt.pdf**.

Leaf prints

This project shows you how to make a printed leaf border for a picture or poem.

Top tips
- Make a test print on scratch paper first.
- Leave one color to dry before you add the next.

1 To make the border, draw a straight line 2½ inches in from each side of your sheet of construction paper or posterboard. Ask an adult to cut out the middle section for you.

2 Paint the underside of a leaf and press it onto the frame in one corner.

3 Use the same leaf to make prints in the other corners. Coat the leaf with fresh paint each time.

When your border is dry, glue your picture or poem behind it, or use it as a photo frame.

You will need:
- A selection of clean, dry leaves
- Construction paper or posterboard, 12 x 10 inches
- Poster paints
- Paintbrush

4 Build up a **pattern** of leaf shapes in different colors all around the frame. Try beech, sycamore, and oak leaves.

Nature prints

Flowers printed from a real flower head

Stems printed from twigs

Try making prints with:
- ★ Twigs and bark
- ★ Flowers
- ★ The underside of a mushroom

Click for Art!

To see leaf designs by William Morris, visit **www.morrissociety.org**. Click on the designs and follow the links.

Junk prints

Pieces of junk, such as nails, screws, cardboard, or thread spools, make great prints. But always ask before you use them!

Here are some things to try:
★ Corrugated cardboard
★ An empty toilet-paper roll
★ A scrunched-up paper bag
★ Nails, screws, or washers
★ An old sponge or cork
★ A jigsaw-puzzle piece

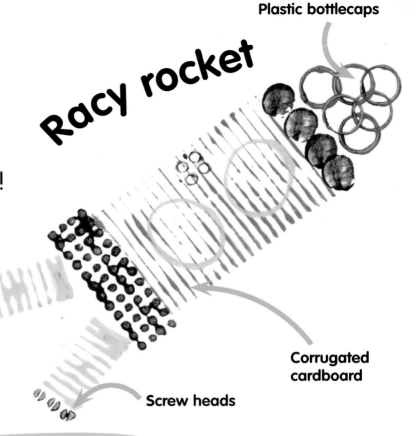

Racy rocket

Plastic bottlecaps

Corrugated cardboard

Screw heads

How to make a printing pad

Printing pads use less paint and make a clearer, cleaner print.

Top tip
Don't forget that you will need to make a separate pad for each color.

1 Ask an adult to help you cut a piece of foam to fit in the bottom of a plastic bowl. The easiest way is to place the bowl on top of the foam and draw around it first.

2 Put the foam into the bottom of the bowl and pour over enough paint to cover it. Leave it until the foam soaks up the paint.

94

stamping robot

Build up your picture from pieces of junk. Print the junk on scratch paper first to see how it looks.

Cork

Corrugated cardboard

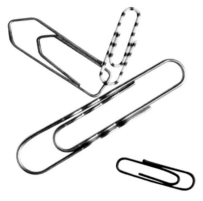

Bubble wrap

Plastic toy brick

3 Press your piece of junk onto the foam, and then press it onto a sheet of paper to make your print.

95

Food prints

Print with fruit or vegetables onto fabric to make fun placemats. Ask an adult to help you with cutting and slicing your food.

Food shapes and patterns

Look for food with interesting **patterns** or shapes:

★ Dried pasta shapes, such as wheels, long tubes, or butterflies

★ A piece of broccoli or cauliflower

★ Half an apple or orange

★ A large cabbage leaf

★ A slice of carrot or celery

★ Half a bell pepper

1 Set out the food you are going to print with, and some dishes of fabric paint. Sketch your rough design on scratch paper first.

2 Ask an adult to help you cut the fabric for the placemats into rectangles of 12 x 10 inches. Use pinking shears so the edges don't fray.

Fabric paints
- Be sure to let each color dry before you add an overlapping one.
- Most fabric paints need to be set with heat to keep the colors from washing out. Ask an adult to press the painted fabric for you by using a hot iron.

Click for Art!

To learn all about traditional block printing on fabric in India, go to **www.sashaworld.com/block/block.htm**.

Top tip

Wipe the cut surface of fruit or vegetables dry before you paint them. This helps the paint stick better— and you will make a clearer print.

3 Dip the food into the paint, or paint the surface of the food with a brush. Press down firmly on the cloth to make the print.

Aztec serpent stamp

Snakes were a symbol of the Aztec god Quetzalcoatl (keht-sal-coh-ah-tl). His name means "feathered serpent."

An Aztec pendant shaped like a two-headed snake. It is made of turquoise (a semiprecious stone) with carved shells for teeth.

An Aztec man (right) and woman (left) say prayers in front of a holy statue. This picture was painted 500 years after the Aztecs lived, but shows us what they looked like.

You will need:
- Two rectangles of cardboard
- Pencil
- Tracing paper
- Craft knife
- Glue
- White, green, and blue acrylic paint
- Saucer
- Paintbrush or roller
- Fine paintbrush
- White paper

Did you Know?
The Aztecs' own name for themselves was the Mexica. Today, we still use this name for their homeland, Mexico.

1 Trace the two-headed snake onto one of the cardboard rectangles. Ask an adult to cut it out with a craft knife.

2 To make your stamp, glue the snake shape to the other card rectangle. Leave to dry completely.

3 Mix up some turquoise paint. Roll or brush paint evenly over the snake shape on your stamp.

4 Turn the block over and press down firmly onto white paper. Gently peel away the card to reveal the snake.

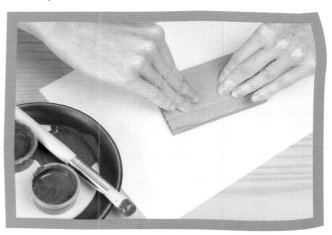

5 Let your snake image dry, then add highlights, such as the eyes, with white paint and a fine paintbrush.

You can use your stamp over and over again!

String prints

Make simple printing blocks by gluing string to small pieces of cardboard or wood. The results are amazing!

You will need:
- Paper or posterboard
- Piece of wood, cardboard, or styrofoam for the printing block
- String
- Poster paints
- Paintbrush

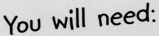

I Paint a blue watery **background** onto paper or posterboard.

2 When the paint is dry, print tall green reeds with the edge of a long piece of cardboard.

Top tip
Sprinkle a little salt onto the blue paint while wet. This will give the background an interesting grainy texture.

3 Glue string to the printing block in a fish shape. Make a large fish block and a smaller one.

4 Glue on string for the fish's scales. Make an eye from string glued in a spiral or a circle of foam.

5 Paint the printing block and press onto the **background**. Paint the block each time you print.

Print fish swimming in the same direction, like real fish.

Print reeds behind and on top of the fish, so the fish appear to be swimming through them.

Simple blocks

You can glue all kinds of things to wood or cardboard to make printing blocks:

★ Grains of rice
★ Nails, screws, or washers
★ Buttons
★ Feathers
★ Paper clips
★ Old keys

Stencil prints

Cards decorated with **stencils** are easy to make—and fun to send to your friends!

You will need:

- Plain and colored cardboard
- Card stock for the stencil
- Thick paintbrush
- Poster paints

1 Choose a shape that is **symmetrical**—the same on both sides.

2 Fold a small square of card stock in half. Draw half the design at the fold.

3 Carefully cut out your **stencil** and open it out.

4 Fold a sheet of colored cardboard in half lengthwise.

5 Hold your stencil firmly over the front of the card and dab paint through the stencil with a thick, bristly brush.

Top tip
Use a little paint at a time so that it does not leak under the stencil.

Wrapping paper and gift tags

Print stencils in a regular **pattern** onto plain paper to make a sheet of wrapping paper.

Print a stencil onto a square of cardboard and punch a hole in it to make a matching gift tag.

Click for Art!

To see stencils by Yoshitoshi Mori, go to **www.castlefinearts.com/catalog.aspx?catID=97**.

Marbling

In marbling, a beautiful print is made from swirling oil paint dripped into water. Oil and water don't mix, so the oil paint stays on the surface of the water and sticks to the paper when it is gently laid on top.

1 Fill your bowl or pan almost to the top with water.

2 With an adult's help, mix the paint and mineral spirits until the paint is runny. ⚠️

Top tip
When marbling, use just two colors to start with. If you use too many, they will mix together and become muddy.

Marbled collage
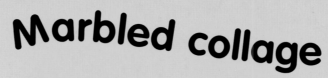
Cut shapes of marbled paper and stick them onto a **background** of different-colored paper so the pictures stand out.

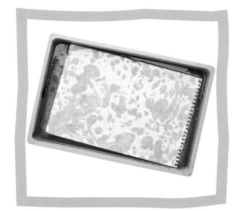

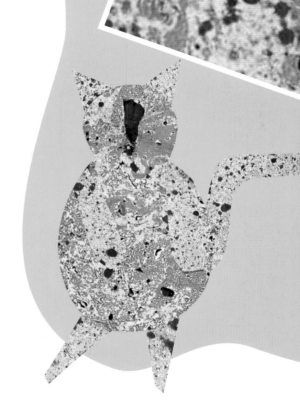

3 Drop tiny blobs of paint onto the water's surface and gently swirl the colors around with a pencil or a stick.

4 Lay your paper on the water's surface. Make sure there are no air bubbles trapped underneath the paper.

Top tip
Instead of stirring the paint with a pencil, try blowing it around the bowl through a straw.

5 Leave for a few seconds, then gently remove the paper. Place the marbled paper on a flat surface to dry.

Click for Art!
To see beautiful examples of marbled paper, go to **http://members.aol.com/marbling/marbling**. Click on "34 Samples of Marbling."

Mirror printing

This is one of the simplest and quickest ways to print. The method is always the same, but every print is different.

Easy butterfly print

1 Fold the paper in half. Open it out and paint some thick blobs on one side, roughly in the shape of half a butterfly. Make sure the paint goes right into the fold, but not over it.

2 Fold the paper over. Press down firmly, and then open it up.

Top tip
This works well for **symmetrical** shapes, such as flowers or leaves. See how many designs you can come up with.

Top tip
Experiment with strings of different thicknesses and **textures**.

String prints

String prints make fascinating swirly patterns.

You will need:
- Paper
- Poster paints
- Saucers
- String
- Scissors

1 Cut three lengths of string. Put three different-colored poster paints into separate saucers. Put a piece of string in each saucer. Make sure the strings are well coated with paint.

2 Fold a piece of paper in half, then open it back out, as you did for the mirror print. Lay the strings carefully on one side of the paper, with one end of each string sticking out over the edge.

3 Fold the other half of the paper over again and press your hand firmly over the surface. Keeping your hand pressed down, pull out the strings by their ends. Open the paper to see your swirly string picture!

Cardboard prints

One of the most common methods of printing is to use blocks. These can be simple or complex. You can make your own blocks for printing—the easiest to make are simple shapes cut out of cardboard.

Print kit

Save as many different types of cardboard as possible—**corrugated** is great for striped, **textured** prints. You can use all parts of the cardboard—the smooth sides are good for printing blocks of color, while the edges are useful for lines and curves. Use the ends of straws or cardboard tubes to make circles or ovals.

Top tip
To make your blocks easier to use, glue a small piece of cork or Styrofoam to the back to serve as a handle.

Print a greeting card

Try making blocks for a simple greeting card. You can reuse them to make a batch of cards—perfect for Christmas.

You will need:
- Poster paints
- Paintbrush
- Cardboard and paper
- Scissors

1 Sketch out your ideas for the card design on scrap paper. Keep the shapes simple.

2 Now cut out the shapes you need for your design. You can glue small pieces of Styrofoam to the back to serve as handles.

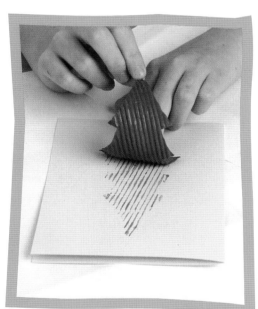

3 Brush the largest printing block with paint. Now press it firmly onto the paper and peel it off to reveal the print beneath.

4 When the first color is dry, do the same with the smaller blocks until your picture is finished. Try not to smudge!

5 You can add details by printing with the tops of pen lids.

Top tip

When you make a print, remember that the finished print will be a mirror image of your printing block.

Making blocks

By gluing objects to small pieces of wood, you can make printing blocks that you can use over and over again. See what objects you can find around the house to add to your printing blocks.

Simple kit

Glue string to small pieces of wood or heavyweight cardboard in interesting shapes for simple prints.

Try making shapes from foam, rubber, sponge, old keys, paper clips, dried pasta, buttons, buckles, old toys, or broken jewelry. Almost anything will work!

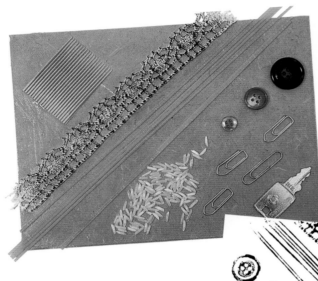

Let your imagination run wild—but don't forget to ask permission first.

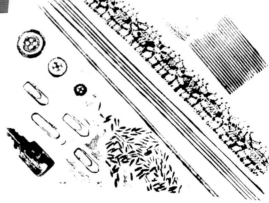

You can paint on lots of bright colors to get a rainbow effect.

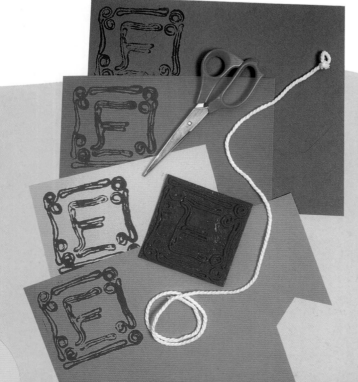

Make a bookplate

Glue string onto one side of a block of wood to form the shape of your initial (be sure to do it in reversed writing). Add a few decorations, and use it to print your initial on the front page of your books. You could also use it to make personalized notepaper.

Sponge stamps

These are ideal for crisp, clean prints. You can buy them at a store, but it is fun to make your own.

1 Draw a simple design on the soft side of the sponge.

2 Ask an adult to cut away the parts around the design using a craft knife.

3 Brush or roll paint over the raised surface and then press the stamp down onto the paper.

Sponges are also great for smaller patterns, such as wallpaper for a dollhouse. You could even make some stamps for adding colorful designs to your letters.

Try printing a trail of animal tracks. Glue thin stamps around the outside of a stiff cardboard tube, and use it as a roller printer.

You will need:
- Sponge
- Craft knife
- Paintbrush
- Poster paint
- Paper

111

Prints from nature

Some of the most delicate prints are made using natural objects. Feathers, leaves, flowers, and wood all make intricate designs. Using prints, you can make a **pattern** that would take hours to paint with a brush.

Print kit

See what natural printers you can find when you are out on a walk. Some, such as feathers and bark, will keep for several years, while green leaves will have to be used before they dry out.

Roll or brush poster paint carefully over leaves, ferns, wheat stalks, etc., and press them onto paper to make a print. Experiment with different effects and colors. For example, a white leaf or fern print looks great on dark paper.

Top tip
Leaves don't last very long, but you can make long-lasting leaf-shaped printers! Just trace around leaves onto heavyweight cardboard, cut them out, and use them as printing blocks.

Leaf prints

Choose three different types of leaves and brush each one with a different color of paint to print a pattern.

1 Brush a bright color over one of the leaves, and press it down onto dark-colored paper. Do this several times, then let the paint dry.

2 Use a different color of paint for the second leaf. Print onto the paper, overlapping the first leaf prints.

3 Continue printing until hardly any of the dark **background** shows through.

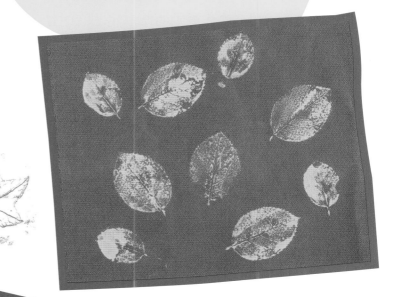

Mount your picture on colored paper and place it on your wall.

Top tip
Try printing while the first color is still wet. Use pastel colors on white paper for an airy, delicate effect.

Potato prints

A potato print is a unique way of making a print with food.

Print kit

All you need to make a potato printer is a big potato and a craft knife. Your printer won't last very long, but if you slice off the old design, you can start again on the fresh surface. Other root vegetables (such as carrots and ginger) make good printing blocks, too—try a few and see which ones work best.

You will need:
- Large potato
- Sharp pencil
- Craft knife
- Poster paints
- Paper

1 Ask an adult to cut the potato in half. Draw a simple design on the cut surface with a sharp pencil. Try a butterfly, a flower, or a star.

2 Ask an adult to cut around the design and remove the excess from the edges so your design sticks out. Brush paint over the surface of the design.

3 Press the painted surface firmly onto paper. Rock the printer gently, so that all parts of the design touch the paper.

Try colored paper and contrasting paints for attractive gift wrap.

Your friends and family will enjoy receiving a handmade gift tag with your own design on it.

Top tip
It's fun to make your own gift tags. Cut lots of small rectangles from colored cardboard and fold them in half. Punch a hole in the top-left corner to thread some ribbon through. Then use potato printers to make a design. You could make an interesting border around the edges, too.

Top tip
Use a cookie cutter to make an instant printer! Just press the cutter into a potato, and ask an adult to cut away around the outside before removing the cutter.

Top tip
Try using different-colored paints on different parts of a butterfly to get some really interesting multicolored results!

Make a Pop Art print

The artist **Andy Warhol** often repeated the same image several times to make bold, bright paintings and prints. Here's how to make a really striking Warhol-style Pop Art print for your wall.

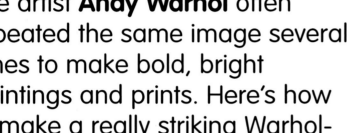

1 Brush brightly colored paint over the bubble pack, and press it down onto the paper to print a dotted pattern. Do this several times, and use a different color for each piece of paper. Use the ruler and pencil to cut the prints into neat squares, each the same size.

2 Glue the squares to a piece of cardboard to make a **checkered** effect. Leave a wide border. Brush paint over your printer and press it onto the first square—choose a color that contrasts with the dots. Red and green, blue and orange, and yellow and purple all make good contrasts.

116

3 Continue printing onto the squares until each one is filled. Use the black felt-tip pen to go over the lines of each square. Cut some cardboard to make a **frame**. Paint it in a bright color and then cut a wavy **outline** with scissors. Tape a loop of yarn to the back so that you can hang it up.

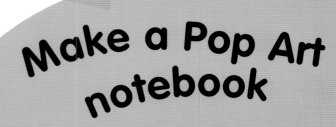

The dots in your picture will make it look like the prints that Andy Warhol made.

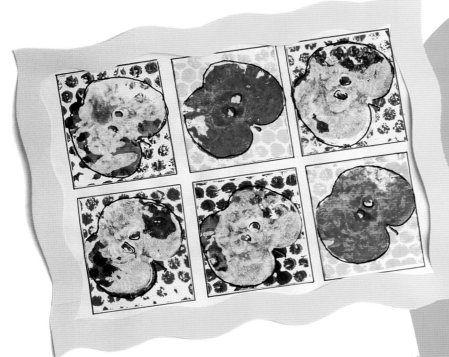

Make a Pop Art notebook

Protect the print with adhesive plastic. Place an open notebook on the back of the print, and draw around it. Draw a border of 2 inches. Cut flaps in the border, and fold them over the covers of the book, gluing them in place. Glue the first and last pages of the notebook to the covers, to hide the flaps.

Monoprints

A monoprint is made by pressing a piece of paper over a painted design and lifting it off. The **textures** and shapes you get would be impossible to create by painting—they may not always be successful, but when they are, they can be great!

Print kit

You will need a really smooth surface to print from—a piece of formica, a mirror, or a shiny baking sheet are ideal. Water-based printing inks give the best effects, but you can also use thick paint. Mix the paint with a little dishwashing detergent and white school glue to keep it from drying out too quickly. As with the mirror prints on page 106, a monoprint (meaning "one print") can never be repeated.

Top tip

When you roll your paint out onto the flat surface, try mixing two colors together to create an interesting graduation between one color and the next. Experiment with multicolored monoprints, using lots of different colors.

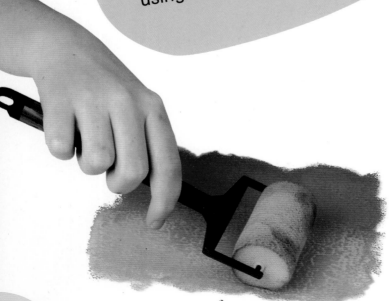

Take care!

Be careful if you are using glass to print on—you will need adult help. Check with an adult before you use a table or other piece of furniture to make your monoprint.

Drawing a monoprint

In this project, you draw a shape to create a monoprint beneath.

You will need:
- Thick paint or printing ink
- A smooth surface
- Roller or wide paintbrush
- Paper

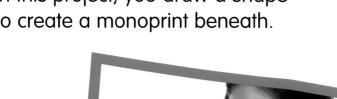

1 Roll bands of color onto the smooth surface, and place the paper lightly on top.

2 Using a pencil, crayon, or knitting needle, draw a design on the paper—try to press the paper just on the lines you are drawing.

3 Lift up the paper gently, making sure not smudge the image. Let it dry out completely.

Stencils

Stenciling was very popular among the early pioneers, who couldn't buy wallpaper or decorated furniture. Practice stenciling on paper or cardboard first—when you feel confident enough, you could use the stencils to decorate your bedroom.

What you need:
- Rigid stencil paper or thin cardboard
- Short-haired paintbrush
- Thick paint
- Pencil
- Craft knife
- Paper

Print kit

There are plenty of premade stencils to use for printing that you can find in craft stores. You will need a brush with short, stubby bristles to work with stencils. The paint should be almost dry, and you should dab it over the stencil. This technique is called "stippling."

1 Draw a simple design onto stencil paper or cardboard with a pencil.

2 Ask an adult to cut out the shapes with a craft knife.

3 Tape the stencil to the sheet of paper. Using an almost-dry brush, stipple the paint over the hole in the stencil, making sure that you go right up to the edges.

Stencil spatter

Instead of stippling your stencil design, you can spatter! Just load the paint onto an old toothbrush, point the brush at the paper, and run cardboard over the bristles. Use interesting shapes such as leaves, keys, or tools. What happens if you move them slightly, and then spatter again with another color?

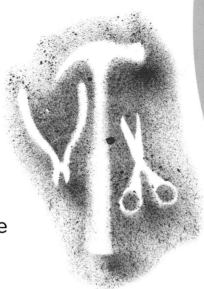

Top tip
Use a simple stenciled design to decorate writing paper and matching envelopes. You could also make stencil gift wrap—use spray paint for really quick results.

Spray stenciling

For really quick stenciling, you could use spray paint. Spray paints come in lots of interesting colors, such as the silver used here.

Top tip
You can use your stencils to decorate lots of personal belongings. Ask an adult for help with cutting.

1 Make a large stencil with a repeat **pattern**. Place it over colored paper and spray paint over it.

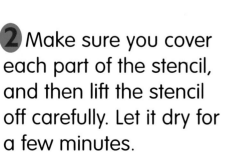

2 Make sure you cover each part of the stencil, and then lift the stencil off carefully. Let it dry for a few minutes.

Printing pictures

The more you experiment with different kinds of printers, the more ideas you are likely to get for your pictures. You can mix prints with **collage** and paint effects, too. Try to think about your prints in a new way—a cabbage leaf print may look just like a cabbage leaf, but it would also make a great tree!

You will need:
- Cabbage leaves
- Thick paints
- Thin, watered-down paints
- Paintbrushes
- Paper
- Thick paper
- Glue
- Scissors

Trees in the park

In this project, you can use cabbage leaves to create intricate tree shapes that would take a long time to draw or paint.

1 Paint the background very quickly, using a wide, soft brush and thin, watered-down paints. Let it dry. (Taping it down to your work surface prevents the paper from wrinkling.)

2 Now make lots of tree prints, using cabbage leaves of different sizes. Use a good variety of colors, from yellow-green to greens with a brown or bluish shade.

A stippling brush (one with short, stiff bristles) is good for brushing paint onto the cabbage leaf.

122

3 When the "trees" are dry, cut them out and glue them to the picture. Finish the picture by printing the fence, using the edge of a piece of cardboard brushed with brown paint.

Can you make a print collage like this of your favorite view? How about a fantasy landscape—such as a spaceship landing on a distant planet?

Top tip
Cauliflower and broccoli make good trees, too. Simple shapes torn from paper make delicate clouds, misty mountains, icebergs, or rough rocks. Sandpaper is perfect for cliffs.

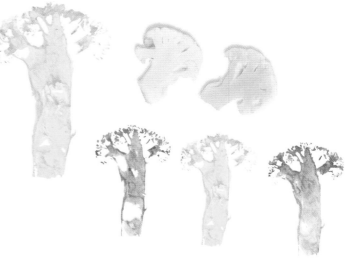

Materials kit

This section will show you how to make amazing crafts from around the world. On this page you can see most of the things you need to get going. Some extras are listed with each project.

1   Sticky tape or masking tape
2   Glue stick
3   Dish of wallpaper paste for papier-mâché projects
4   Balloons
5   Paintbrushes
6   Paper fasteners
7   Poster paints
8   Air-drying modeling clay
9   Enamel paint
10 Beads, stick-on gems, sequins, etc.
11 Colored paper
12 Paint roller
13 Crayons and colored chalk
14 Pencils
15 Ruler
16 Safety scissors
17 String
18 Tissue paper
19 Sketching pad
20 Cutting board
21 Pencil sharpener

Paints and paintbrushes

In addition to different colors of poster paint, you will need some white latex paint for first coats on clay or papier-mâché models. You also need a selection of paintbrushes: a small decorating brush (for glue or to paint large areas), a medium-size brush, and a thin brush for fine detail.

Craft foam

Craft foam is useful for all kinds of projects. You can buy sheets of brightly colored craft foam. Some craft stores also sell bags of precut foam squares and shapes.

African cloth picture

In Benin, Africa, people tell stories with brightly colored cloth pictures. You can make your own picture using **felt.**

A long time ago, cloth pictures like these hung behind the throne of the king of Benin.

You will need:
- Felt (black, red, yellow, orange)

Ask an adult to help you enlarge these animal shapes on a photocopier.

1 Draw an animal with a felt-tip pen on the back of a piece of felt. Ask an adult to help you cut it out.

Click for Art!

To see traditional cloth pictures from Benin, visit **www.kidstoafrika.org/benin/tapestries**.

Top tip
Cut scraps of different-colored felt and glue them onto your animal shape.

2 Ask an adult to help you cut out a piece of black felt for your background. Make it at least 2 inches bigger than your felt shape.

3 Cut out four strips of colored felt 1 inch wide to make a frame. Overlap the strips at each corner and glue them in place.

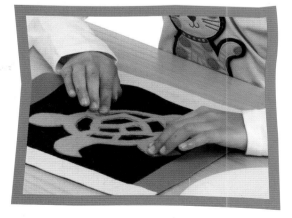

4 Glue your animal picture in the middle of the black background.

127

Egyptian collar

Neck collars were made from semiprecious stones or gold, clay, or glass beads. How many pretty bits and pieces can you find for yours?

Put your collar on and tie at the back. For a real Egyptian look, you could add a thin headband!

Queen Nefertiti wore tight, patterned robes, which were fashionable around 1500 BC. She also wore thick eyeliner, a heavy jeweled collar, and bracelets on both arms.

You will need:

- 16-inch square of felt
- Compass and pencil
- Scissors
- Glue
- Beads, gems, buttons, sequins, and felt scraps
- Red ribbon

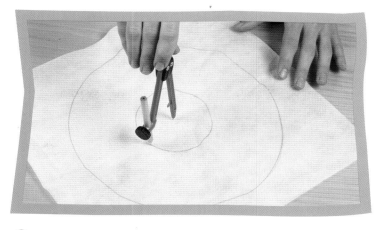

1 Set your compass to 5 inches and draw a circle. Set it to 1½ inches. Draw another circle from the same point.

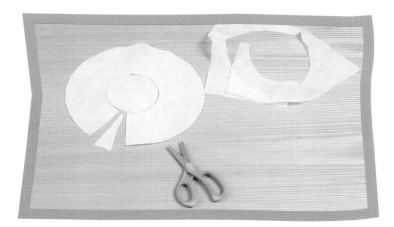

2 Cut both circles out and then cut away a small section of the collar shape, as shown here.

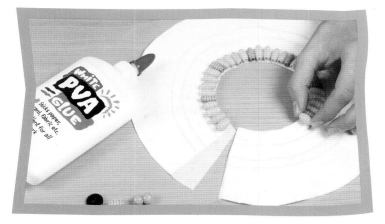

3 Put a line of glue around the inside of the collar and place different-colored beads along it.

4 Add another line of glue and more buttons. Continue to build up the pattern in this way.

5 On each side of the collar, glue one end of a length of red ribbon to the felt backing.

Roman robe clasp

Romans did not have zippers or buttons. They used clasps and brooches instead. Make a stunning dog clasp for your Roman robe!

This dog-shaped brooch was used to fasten a Roman robe. It is made of bronze and decorated with enamel (colored glass).

Did you know?

Roman women wore wigs! The wigs were made from dark hair purchased from India or from blonde hair cut from German captives and slaves.

You will need:

- Pencil
- Tracing paper
- White pencil
- Black card stock
- Scraps of gold foil
- Scissors
- Glue
- Colored paper
- Gold pen
- Safety pin
- Tape
- Fine-tip black marker

Roman women wore their long hair arranged in many sophisticated styles. Roman men were clean shaven with short hair, except around AD 100–200, when they preferred longer curls and beards.

1 Draw or trace the dog shape onto black card stock and go over it in white pencil. Cut it out with scissors.

2 Draw the body shape and eye on gold foil and cut out. Now glue them onto your black dog shape.

3 Cut out small shapes from colored paper. Arrange and then glue them onto the gold panel.

4 Use a gold pen to add teeth, a collar, and details to the ears and legs. Draw a solid black circle on the eye.

Romans used clasps to hold their cloaks together, but you could pin yours to a white sheet worn as a toga.

5 Use a small piece of masking tape to attach a safety pin to the back of your cloak clasp.

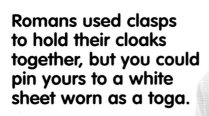

131

Aboriginal painting

This project shows you how to paint a dot picture in the style of the Australian Aboriginal people.

1 Paint the whole paper pale yellow or orange. Leave it to dry.

2 Ask an adult to help you copy the lizard shape below onto your picture. Paint it a rich, rusty red. Add wavy lines around it in dark orange or red and allow it to dry.

3 Dip a cotton swab in white or yellow paint. Print rows of dots on the lizard's back and on some of the wavy lines.

You will need:
- Acrylic or poster paints in rich, warm colors
- Cotton swabs

Click for Art!

For examples of Aboriginal dot paintings, go to **www.thebritishmuseum.ac.uk/compass** and search for "Aboriginal art."

4 Paint large orange or red circles around the lizard. When the paint is dry, print red, black, or brown and white dots on the circles.

Lively dot patterns and warm, earthy colors are typical of Aboriginal art.

Top tip
Arrange blobs of different-colored paint in saucers. Use a different cotton swab for each color.

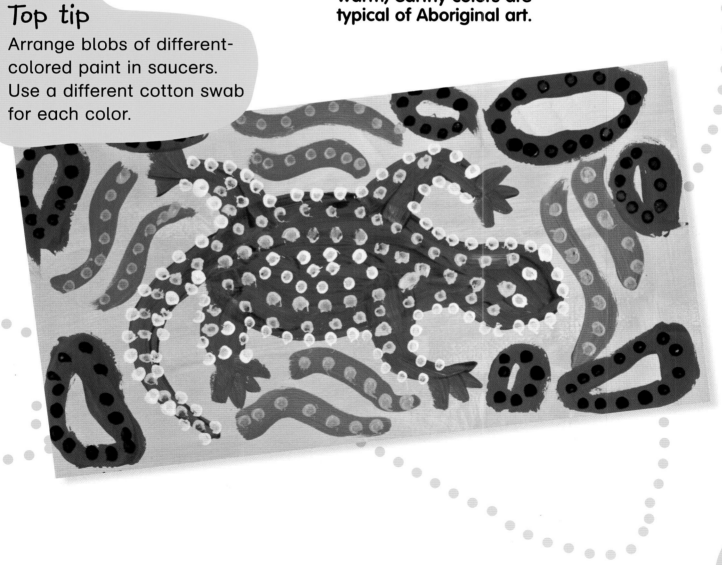

Roman laurel leaf crown

Make a laurel leaf crown and dress up as an all-powerful emperor. Remind everyone that the emperor's word is law!

Laurel leaf crowns were symbols of victory and divine power. Emperors and top athletes wore them.

You will need:

- 4 pipe cleaners
- Thin green card stock
- Ruler
- Pencil
- Scissors
- Masking tape
- Cardboard
- Thin turquoise card stock
- Glue stick

Did you know?

Emperor Caligula (AD 12–41) made his horse prime minister. Emperor Nero (AD 37–68) set fire to Rome, then sang as he watched it burn.

Before a Roman feast, slaves helped guests take off their outdoor clothes— and washed their feet!

1 Twist four pipe cleaners together in a row. Cut out a ¾-inch-wide strip of the same length from green card stock.

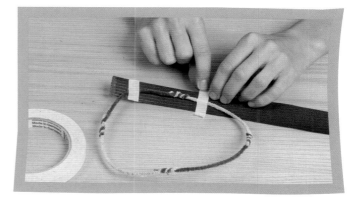

2 Twist together the ends of the pipe cleaners to make a loop. Use masking tape to attach the strip.

3 Draw a leaf onto cardboard and cut it out. This will be your template for step 4.

4 **Accordion-fold** a strip of card stock. Draw around the template onto it. Cut the shape out, cutting through all the layers.

Be a good emperor— honest, wise, and fair.

5 Stick each leaf to the crown with glue. Repeat step 4 to make as many leaves as you need to cover the ring.

135

Roman serpent arm bracelet

Swirling snake bracelets were popular with Roman women. Snakes were a symbol of good health for a woman and her family. They were also painted on walls and added to mosaic floor patterns.

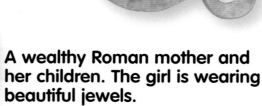

A wealthy Roman mother and her children. The girl is wearing beautiful jewels.

You will need:

- 2 pipe cleaners
- Ruler
- Pencil
- Gold card stock
- Scissors
- Masking tape
- Glue
- Fine-tip black marker

1 Twist two pipe cleaners together. Measure the length of the two pipe cleaners.

2 Draw two rectangles on gold card stock that are each the same length as the pipe cleaners and ½ inch wide.

3 Use masking tape to attach the pipe cleaners to the back of one rectangle. Glue the other on top.

4 Using the black marker, draw a snake's head. Then add the body and swirly tail.

Wear your serpent on your upper arm like a Roman!

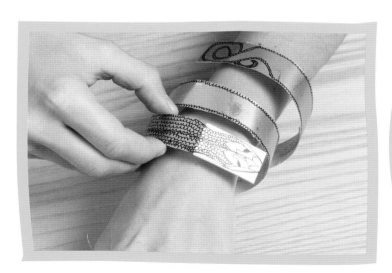

5 Curl the snake around your lower arm. When it's the right shape, you can push it to the top of your arm.

Chinese paper dragon

At New Year, Chinese people dance in the street with huge paper and cloth dragons. Here's how to make a puppet dragon.

1 Trace the dragon's head and tail onto tracing paper, then onto cardboard. Ask an adult to help you cut out the shapes.

2 Paint both sides of a sheet of white paper bright red. When dry, fold the paper in half lengthwise and cut along the fold.

3 Fold the pieces of paper to form an **accordion**. Glue the two pieces of paper together to make one long piece for the dragon's body.

Ask an adult to enlarge these shapes on a photocopier.

Click for Art!

To learn about dragons in ancient China, go to the Web site **www.chinapage.com/dragon1.html**.

The dragon dance is performed at Chinese New Year to bring good luck.

Googly eye

4 Paint the dragon's head and tail in bright colors, and glue on sequins, glitter, and a googly eye.

5 Glue the head and tail to the dragon's body with craft glue.

6 Glue the chopsticks or Popsicle sticks to the head and tail of the dragon.

Dye material the Viking way

Vikings used berries and vegetables to dye material beautiful colors. Their dyeing technique still works 1,000 years later!

This rich Viking man is wearing a cozy fur hat, a thick wool cloak, and fur-lined leather boots.

You will need:

- 2 pounds of raw beets
- Knife
- Cutting board
- Rubber gloves
- Saucepan
- 3.3 feet of cotton tape
- White cotton T-shirt
- Wooden spoon
- Colander
- Acrylic paint
- Paintbrushes
- Double-sided tape

Did you know?

Vikings bathed at least once a week—usually on a Saturday—by having a sauna (a bath in clouds of steam). This amazed the English, who washed less often.

1 Chop the beets and put them in a saucepan half-filled with cold water. Remember to wear rubber gloves.

2 Put in the tape and T-shirt. Ask an adult to bring it to a boil. Simmer for one hour, stirring occasionally.

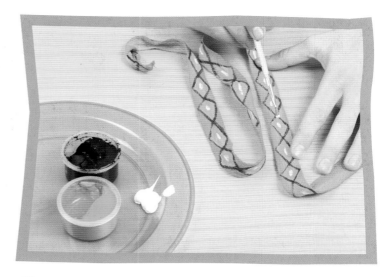

3 When cool, strain through a colander. Then remove the tape and T-shirt from the beet pulp.

4 Rinse well and hang up to drip dry. Once the tape's dry, paint a Viking pattern along it.

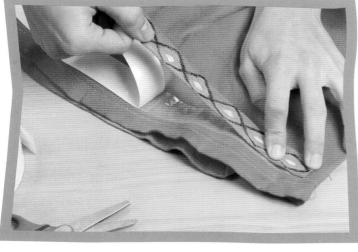

5 When the T-shirt and tape are dry, stick or sew the tape to the T-shirt.

Feel like a proud Viking in your bright, patterned top. (Don't forget that your top is not colorfast and should always be washed separately.)

Mexican Metapec sun

Mexican craftspeople make beautiful clay pottery. Here's how to make a Metapec clay sun to hang on your wall.

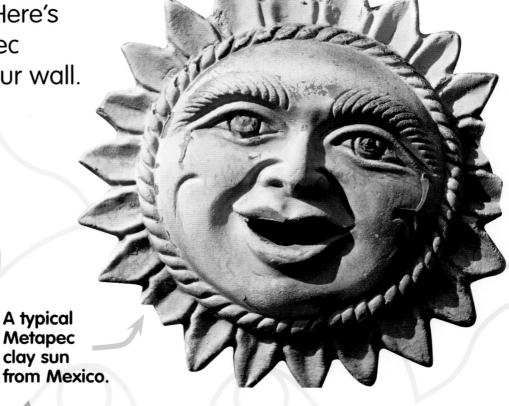

You will need:
- Air-drying clay
- Rolling pin
- Mixing bowl
- Blunt kitchen knife
- Bright acrylic or poster paints
- Paintbrushes
- String or twine

A typical Metapec clay sun from Mexico.

1 Soften the clay in your hands, then flatten it with a rolling pin. It needs to be about ½ inch thick and a bit bigger than your mixing bowl.

2 Place a mixing bowl over the clay. Ask an adult to help you cut around the bowl with a dull knife.

3 Make holes for the eyes and mouth. Make clay eyes and eyebrows, a nose, and mouth, and stick them on with a little water.

4 Make clay rays to go around your sun's face. Press them firmly into place or stick them on with a little water.

5 Push a pencil through the top of the sun to make a hole for the string.

6 Let your sun harden, then paint it in bright colors. Thread string through the hole at the top so you can hang it on the wall.

Top tip

To make your clay sun look shiny, paint it with white school glue mixed with water. The glue looks white when wet, but will be clear and shiny when it is dry.

Ancient world art

Thousands of years ago in the Stone Age, people produced some fantastic paintings. Many were made in caves—possibly as decorations for ceremonies or on religious shrines. Follow the steps below to re-create a magical Stone Age animal painting.

You will need:
- Air-drying clay
- Rolling pin
- Sand
- Poster paint
- Black charcoal (optional)
- Cotton balls
- Sandpaper
- Varnish (optional)

A Stone Age cave painting

1 Lightly draw an animal outline, such as a cow, deer, bison, or elephant, on scrap paper. Use a soft pencil and keep the lines simple.

Top tip
Draw the animal's legs at an angle, not straight down, so it looks as though it is running.

2 Roll out a piece of pale modeling clay (the size of a tennis ball). It doesn't have to be totally smooth. Rub some sand over the clay for a rough surface texture. Then let the clay dry hard.

3 Squirt black and white paint into two separate pools. Mix some to make a light gray, and use a cotton ball or a piece of foam to dab it onto the clay. When this is dry, paint your animal outline in black.

Top tip

You can seal your painting with white school glue mixed with water instead of varnish. Put some glue in a plastic cup. Gradually add water until it is a creamy consistency. It looks white when you paint it on, but it dries clear.

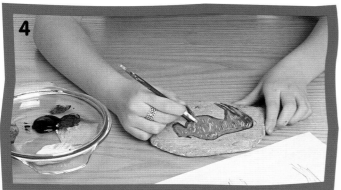

4 Paint the body in natural colors, such as dark browns and reds.

5 When the paint is dry, gently rub sandpaper over the surface to make it look patchy and old.

6 Apply two coats of clear varnish. Let the varnish dry between coats.

Aztec mask

This death mask is guaranteed to frighten your friends. Tezcatlipoca was the Aztec god of night and the future. He was believed to start wars.

Did you know?

An ordinary person wishing to speak to a ruler at the palace had to bow very low and keep their eyes looking down. When they left, they walked backward because it was very rude to face away from the ruler.

This mask is of the god Tezcatlipoca (tess-kah-tlee-poh-ka). It is a real skull covered in a mosaic of semiprecious stones.

No Aztec pyramid temples have survived, but they would have looked like this pyramid, built by earlier Mexican people in the city of Teotihuacan.

You will need:

- Black card stock
- Ruler
- Pencil
- Scissors
- Craft knife
- Silver foil
- Blue, green, turquoise, black, and white paper
- Glue
- Elastic thread
- White felt or card stock

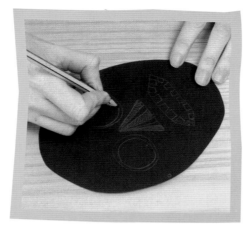

1 Measure your face. On the card stock, draw an oval shape that is big enough to completely cover your face.

2 Draw on the eyes, mouth, and nose. Then ask an adult to cut them out with a craft knife.

3 Glue on two wide strips of foil. Cut out the eyes, nose, and mouth holes. Glue on colored paper shapes.

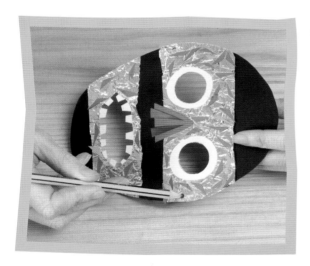

4 Use a sharp pencil to make holes for the elastic at each side of the mask, below the eyes.

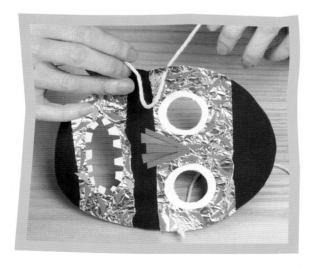

5 Finally, thread elastic through the side holes. Put the mask on. Gently tighten the elastic and knot it to secure the mask.

Put on your mask and imagine that you can see into the future, like a god.

147

Egyptian amulet

The ancient Egyptians believed that people's spirits must be reunited with their bodies after they died. They decorated dead bodies with amulets, or lucky charms. In this project, you can make a wedjat-eye charm, which the Egyptians used to ward off evil spirits.

You will need:

- Air-drying clay
- Rolling pin or bottle
- Plastic knife
- Wooden or plastic modeling tools
- Poster paint
- Varnish

1 Roll out a piece of clay until it is ½ to ¾ inch thick and about ¾ inch larger than you want your finished eye to be. Carve the **outline** of an eye on the clay with a modeling tool or pencil. Cut out the shape with a plastic knife.

Ancient Egyptian scarab (beetle) amulets

2 Roll out long, thin pieces of clay and press them into the eye shape to build up the design.

3 Use your tools to make patterns in the clay for decoration.

Top tip

Everyday household objects, such as a fork, a blunt nail, or the end of a paintbrush, make great tools.

4 When the model is dry, paint it. Once the paint is dry, add a coat of **varnish**. Let this first coat dry and then add another.

Top tip

To get a smooth surface for decorating, paint an undercoat of white latex paint. Let this dry before adding colored poster paint.

Ancient Greek vase

The best pottery in ancient Greece was made in Athens. A vase, like the one below, would have stored oil, wine, or water. The vase in this project is made of papier-mâché, so don't put liquid in it!

You will need:

- Large, oval-shaped balloon
- Newspaper
- Wallpaper paste
- Thin cardboard
- Paint and paintbrushes

1 Blow up the balloon. Mix some wallpaper paste. Tear sheets of newspaper into 1 x 2-inch strips.

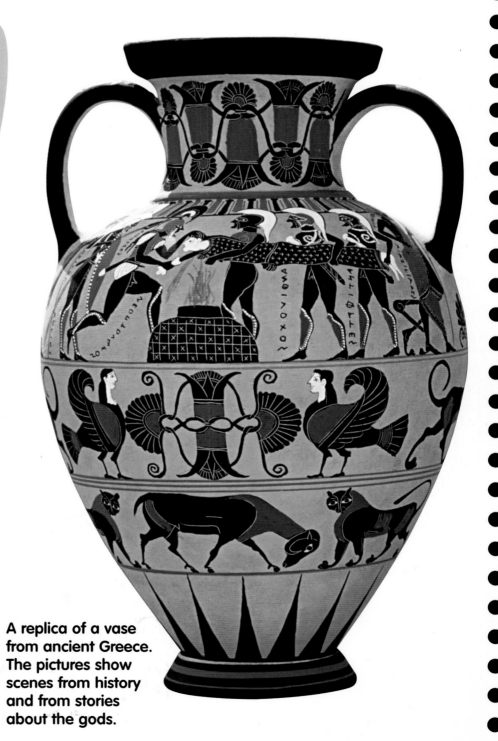

A replica of a vase from ancient Greece. The pictures show scenes from history and from stories about the gods.

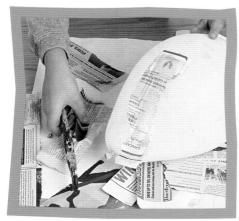

2 Soak the strips in the paste, then lay them over the balloon neatly so they overlap. Cover the balloon in two layers. Let it dry.

3 Repeat until you have eight layers. When the paste is dry, pop the balloon with a pin.

4 Cut out a strip of thin cardboard and tape it in a circle to the base of the balloon shape. Attach a wider piece to the top. Cut two more strips of cardboard and tape them to the sides of the vase for handles.

5 Cover the cardboard base, top, and handles with two layers of strips. Make sure that the strips overlap the main part of the vase. When dry, add another layer.

6 When this is dry, paint the vase reddish-brown. Paint the base, rim, and handles of the vase black.

7 Draw the owl—the symbol of the goddess Athena—on the side. Paint the owl **outline** black. Paint decorative borders on the base and top of your vase. When it is dry, **varnish** the whole vase.

Roman-style mosaic

Many Roman homes had a mosaic—a picture made of tiny glass, stone, or tile squares called "tesserae"—pressed into the floor. Mosaics showed pictures of many different things.

You will need:
- Graph paper
- Colored paper or white paper and poster paints, or old magazines, or gummed colored paper
- Black construction paper
- Scissors
- Glue

1 Plan your design on graph paper so that the finished design is about 6 x 9 inches. Copy this dog mosaic or choose another animal—or your initials. Design a border to frame your design.

Roman mosaics

2

Top tip

Squares cut from magazines give you different **hues** of each of your colors, which gives your design more depth.

2 Put the paper with the design on it facedown on the construction paper. Rub the paper with a pencil to transfer the design to the construction paper.

3 Cut equal-size squares from colored paper. Sort each color into a separate pile: blues, greens, reds, etc.

3

4 Glue the squares onto the construction paper. Leave a thin gap between each square.

5 To make your mosaic shine, paint it with white glue mixed with water.

4

5

Top tip

If you want your mosaic to sparkle, cover some squares in glitter glue or paint them in gold or silver metallic paint.

Indian rangoli

Rangoli is the Indian art of decorating the floor or wall with a **geometric** design, flowers, or animals. Intricate rangoli are painted during Hindu festivals such as Diwali, or for birthdays. Each state of India has its own style of rangoli.

You will need:
- Colored construction paper
- Sketch paper
- Pencil
- White chalk
- Colored chalk (or flour) with food coloring

1 Practice drawing small rangoli on sketch paper. Draw a larger version on a big sheet of paper. Start with a series of evenly spaced dots.

An Indian woman making a rangoli

2 Join some of the dots to form a geometric pattern, a flower, or animal shape. Here are some ideas.

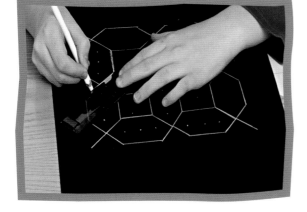

3 Copy your design onto the sidewalk or playground in chalk or in a flour and water paste (always ask permission first), or draw your rangoli on a large sheet of black construction paper.

Top tip
Make sure your dots are evenly spaced so that you end up with a regular pattern.

4 Color your rangoli with chalk. If you use flour paste, divide the paste into separate bowls and add a couple of drops of different food coloring to each.

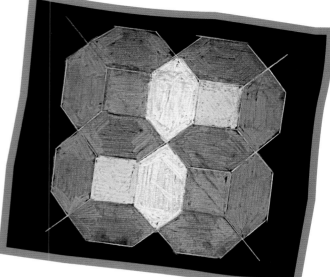

Chinese calligraphy

In China and Japan, calligraphy is an art form. Calligraphers spend months practicing one character, or symbol. The Chinese character on the card in this project means "peace."

You will need:

- Paintbrush and paint (optional)
- Pencil
- Black marker pen
- White heavyweight paper
- Cream heavyweight paper
- Dark heavyweight paper
- Red marker pen
- Ruler
- Scissors

Chinese calligraphy scroll

1 Draw the outline of the "peace" character as shown below, using the graph lines to help you. If you are using a brush, follow the red arrows inside the outlines.

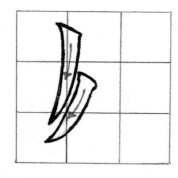   

2 When you have completed the outlines, fill them in with a black marker. Try to keep within your pencil marks.

Top tip

If you use a paintbrush, try different sizes. A thick, pointed brush makes bold, sweeping strokes. Lift the brush away from the paper to make thin, light brushstrokes.

3 Cut out a rectangle of thick, textured cream paper. Fold in half. To make a neat fold, measure where you want the fold to be with a ruler and mark the line in pencil.

4 Color the right edge of the paper in bright red poster paint or marker pen.

5 Cut a piece of dark paper slightly larger than your calligraphy and stick it to the cream paper. Now glue the calligraphy on top, so that a border of dark paper shows through.

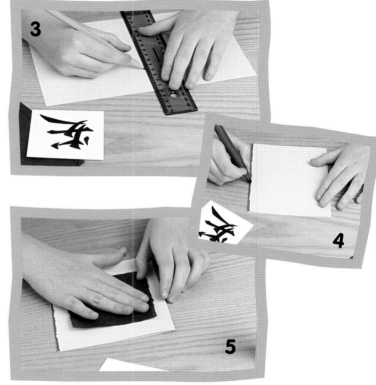

Here are two other Chinese characters to practice. They mean "beautiful" (left) and "lucky" (right).

Aztec warrior outfit

Aztec warriors wore real jaguar skins to show that they shared the strength and fierceness of a big cat. Make a frightening, fake jaguar skin.

Warriors tried to capture enemies alive so that priests could kill them later as sacrifices.

You will need:
- White cotton fabric
- Sewing scissors
- Pencil
- Black marker
- Acrylic or poster paints
- Paintbrushes
- Two pieces of red ribbon

2 In pencil, draw on the body, tail, front legs, and head. Draw dots all over your jaguar's body.

1 Fold the fabric diagonally to make a large triangle. Now cut along the fold.

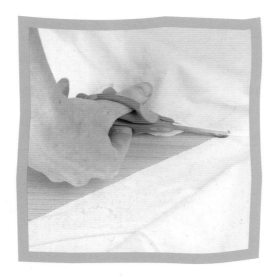

158

3 With a black marker, carefully go over all your pencil lines so the jaguar's features really stand out.

4 Mix up orange paint and color in the jaguar. Don't go over the black lines! Add the spots with black marker.

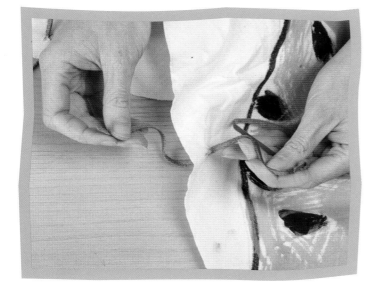

Did you Know?
Jaguar knights were sent on secret missions after dark and would communicate by whistling.

Put on your jaguar cloak and feel strong and brave, just like an Aztec warrior.

5 With scissors, cut a tiny hole on each side of the jaguar's head. Thread red ribbon through each of the holes.

Japanese banner

On Children's Day in Japan, children hang up fish-shaped flags on poles outside their homes to bring them good luck. Here's how to make your own fish banner that you can hang up in your bedroom or classroom.

You will need:
- Colored tissue paper
- Glue
- Scissors
- Thin cardboard

Japanese fish banners

1 Cut three shapes out of tissue paper, copying the shapes in the picture above. Choose a different color for each. The fish will fold along the center, so make sure the pieces are big enough.

Top tip
When cutting out the scales, fold the paper over so that you can cut lots of scales at once.

2 Glue the tail onto one end of the long section, and the head onto the other end.

3 Use your scissors to cut out lots of semicircles of tissue paper for the scales of the fish.

4 Cut out four large circles and two smaller circles to make the eyes. Glue them to the head of the fish.

5 When you have enough scales, add them to the long section of the fish. Glue them from the tail upward, and slightly overlap each row onto the previous one—just like real fish scales.

6 Fold the fish along the center and glue the bottom edges together. Glue a ring of cardboard inside the mouth.

Indonesian puppets

One of the world's oldest traditions of storytelling, shadow puppets, or "wayang kulit," have been popular entertainment in Indonesia for more than 1,000 years. Here's how to make your own Indonesian-style shadow puppet.

You will need:

- Colored construction paper
- Paper
- Cardboard
- Pencil
- Scissors and craft knife
- Paper fasteners
- Wooden dowel or wooden skewers
- Adhesive tape
- White sheet
- Electric light

1 Sketch your puppet design roughly on paper. Give it a long nose; long, curling hair; and a curving body and legs.

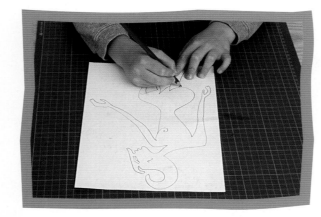

An Indonesian shadow puppet show

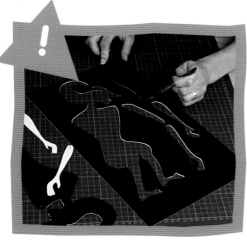

2 When you are happy with your design, draw the figure on cardboard. Draw the arms separately and divide each arm into two parts—shoulder to elbow, and elbow to hand. Round the ends and cut out all the pieces. Ask an adult for help with the craft knife.

3 Tape a stick down the back of one of the puppet's legs, so that the audience cannot see the stick.

4 Join the arms to the body at the shoulder with paper fasteners. Join the lower and upper parts of the arms at the elbow.

5 Tape a thin stick to each of the puppet's hands so that you can move its arms.

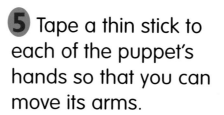

6 To put on a show, suspend a thin white cotton sheet between two chairs. Make sure there are no wrinkles in the sheet. Shine an electric lamp onto the back of the sheet. Kneel down and work the puppet above your head so that your audience sees the puppet's shadow. Use one hand to operate one arm, and the other hand to operate the other arm and the head.

Jarl's helmet

Scandinavian Jarls wore metal helmets to protect their heads and scare their enemies. No one will recognize you behind this helmet!

You will need:
- Balloon
- Newspaper
- Glue mixture (3 parts white school glue, 1 part water)
- Scissors
- White card stock
- Pencil
- Craft knife
- Glue
- Paint and paintbrushes

This detail from the Bayeux Tapestry shows Norman warriors sailing their warships to invade England.

This helmet was designed to give extra protection to the wearer's eyes and nose. The crest on top helped deflect blows to the head.

1 Blow up a balloon. Dip strips of newspaper into the glue mixture. Stick them to the top half of the balloon.

2 Build up several layers of papier-mâché strips. Leave to dry. This may take several hours.

Did you Know?
Viking raiders captured people and then demanded a ransom (blood money) to free them alive.

3 Pop the balloon and remove it. Use scissors to trim the jagged edges all the way around.

4 Draw the eye and nose piece onto card stock. Ask an adult to cut it out with a craft knife.

If you want your helmet to shine, ask an adult to spray paint it for you. Make sure they do it outside!

5 Glue the eye and nose piece to the papier-mâché helmet. When the glue is dry, paint the helmet gold.

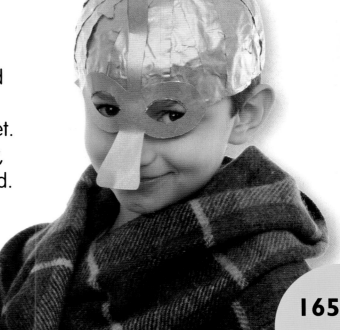

Stained glass

Stained-glass windows decorated churches and cathedrals in medieval times, and still do today. Make your own window and watch it glow when the light streams through it.

You will need:

- Black construction paper
- White pencil
- Craft knife
- Scissors
- Colored tissue paper or colored cellophane
- Glue
- Fine felt-tip black pen

1 Plan your picture first. Keep it simple, using bold lines, and leave a 1- to 2-inch border around it for the frame. Now lightly draw your design on black construction paper with a white pencil. Leave a gap of ¼–½ inch between the different colors.

A medieval stained-glass window

Take care!
You will need an adult to help you with this project.

2 Once you are happy with your design, go over the lines again, this time marking them with bold, white **outlines**.

3 Ask an adult to help you cut out your design with a craft knife. Use a cutting board or several layers of newspaper.

4 Cut tissue paper or cellophane to fit over each window in the paper. Put the pieces in place without glue first to check that they will fit over the holes.

6 Hold the window up to the light. The light will shine through the cellophane, making the colors glow.

5 Glue each piece onto the back of the paper. Put glue around each hole, and try to keep glue off the front of the window.

Top tip
As you cut out more construction paper, the frame becomes fragile. Keep a heavy book over the frame so it does not rip while you cut out the remaining pieces.

Moroccan tile

In countries such as Morocco, **geometric patterns** are used to create beautiful tiles.

You will need:
- Thick cardboard, 5½ inches square
- Craft knife
- Masking tape
- Sponge or roller
- Ceramic paint (oil-based or water-based)
- Turpentine (for oil-based ceramic paints—handle with care!)
- Plain white tile, 6 inches square
- Felt

A Moroccan tile

1 Plan out a tile design and practice drawing it. When you are happy with it, draw it onto your cardboard square.

Top tip
If you use oil-based paint, ask an adult to clean your brushes in turpentine. A cotton ball dipped in turpentine will wipe away mistakes.

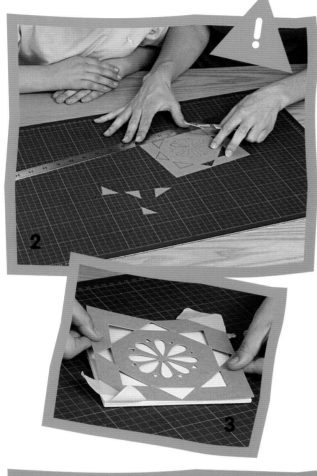

2 Ask an adult to help you cut around the lines with a craft knife. Use a cutting board.

3 Tape the edges of the stencil you have made to a plain white ceramic tile.

4 Dab ceramic paint onto the tile through the stencil with a small sponge, brush, or roller. Try to fill all the gaps with paint.

5 Remove the stencil. Let the paint dry if it is oil-based, or ask an adult to help you to fire it in the oven if it is water-based (follow the instructions on the pack).

6 Cut out a square of felt. Glue it to the back of your tile so that you can put it on a table without scratching it.

169

Papyrus paper

The Egyptians invented paper. They made it from strips of papyrus reed soaked in water, then pressed together. Try making your own!

To make papyrus (the first paper), the Egyptians cut thin strips of papyrus reed stalk, soaked them, laid them flat, then pressed them together.

An Egyptian farmer uses a plow pulled by oxen to prepare his fields for planting crops. His wife walks behind him, scattering seeds on the freshly plowed earth.

You will need:

- Sheet of pale green paper
- Sheet of dark green paper
- Scissors
- Glue mixture (3 parts white school glue, 1 part water)
- Plastic tray
- Paper towels

1 Draw a ½-inch margin along the long edge of one sheet and along the short edge of the other.

2 Cut ½-inch strips across the sheet to the long margin. Cut strips up the other sheet, to the margin.

3 Weave the two pieces of paper together. Weave each strip over, then under, along the row.

4 Fill the plastic tray halfway with the glue mixture. Place your paper completely in the glue mixture.

Did you Know?

Egyptian farmers kept cats to protect their grain stores from rats and mice. The Egyptian word for cat was "miw"!

Impress your friends with your handmade notepaper.

5 Pat your paper with paper towels to remove excess moisture. Hang to dry over a sink or tub.

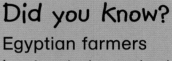

Russian egg

The first Fabergé egg was made in 1885, when the Russian tsar, Alexander III, commissioned a jeweled Easter egg for his wife from the goldsmith Peter Carl Fabergé. Here's how to "blow" a real egg and decorate it in the style of a fabulous Fabergé egg.

You will need:
- Raw egg
- Pin
- Bowl
- Enamel paints
- Dried lentils, peas, or beans
- Stick-on gems

1 Use a pin to make small holes, one through the top and another through the bottom of the egg.

The original Fabergé eggs were made in enamel and decorated with metals such as silver, gold, and copper, and precious stones.

2 Hold the egg over a bowl and gently blow through one of the holes. The contents of the egg will dribble out until the egg is empty.

3 Holding the egg gently, paint the shell.

4 Decorate the egg using lentils, seeds, sequins, or stick-on gems. Carefully dot on glue and press one lentil, seed, sequin, or gem in place at a time.

Top tip
Use tweezers to pick up tiny seeds or gems, dip them in glue (or paint a layer of white glue on the egg first with a brush), and then drop them into place.

Gladiator shield

A gladiator's shield was his best friend—it was the only thing between him and certain death!

You will need:

- Big sheet of cardboard
- Ruler
- Scissors
- Marker
- Paint and paintbrushes
- Compass and pencil
- Double-sided tape
- White card stock

This secutor (which means "pursuer") gladiator wears a heavy helmet and metal leg guards. He is armed with a sharp sword and is protected by a huge, curved shield.

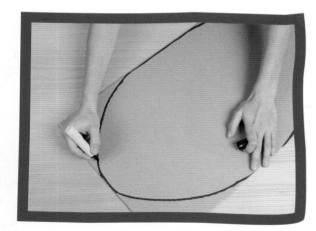

1 Cut a 24 x 16-inch rectangle from cardboard. Inside the rectangle, draw a big oval that touches the edges.

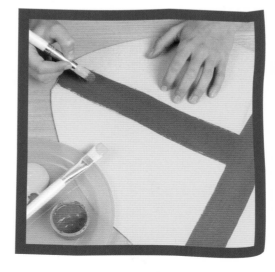

2 Cut out the oval, then paint it yellow and let it dry. Now paint on a red cross, as shown.

There were five different kinds of gladiators. This retarius (which means "net-man") has no helmet or body armor. His only weapons are a spear and a net.

Did you know?
Roman actors invented new plays, called pantomimes, based on comic, acrobatic dances.

4 Draw a circle 4 inches in diameter on card stock using a compass and pencil. Cut it out, paint it brown, and when it's dry, stick it to the center of the shield.

3 Paint two diagonal lines that cross in the middle. Now paint a red border around the rim.

Feel as brave as a gladiator when you carry your shield!

5 Cut out a rectangle of card stock. Use it to make an arm handle on the back, as shown.

Materials kit

In this section you will learn how to make collages, build three-dimensional models, and create unusual effects using a variety of materials, from straws to sequins! Here are some of the things you will need to get started.

Top tip
Don't forget to spread out some newspaper to work on, and wear an apron to keep your clothes clean.

Paper and cardboard
For many of the projects, you will need:
• Thin cardboard or thick white paper
• Colored paper
• Tissue paper
• Construction paper
• Thick cardboard from old boxes
But you can use all kinds of paper in your artwork, such as newspapers and magazines, shiny card stock, tracing paper, crepe paper, brown paper, wallpaper, sandpaper, lacy doilies, used stamps, candy wrappers, paper towels or blotting paper, aluminum foil, bubble wrap, cereal boxes, egg cartons, and paper-towel rolls.

Safety scissors

Other basics

- Safety scissors
- Sticky tape
- Felt-tip pens
- Pencils and ruler
- Wax crayons
- Poster/acrylic paints
- Paintbrushes
- White school glue

You will also need some extra items, which are listed separately for each project.

Bits and pieces

Keep a box of things with interesting textures or shapes. For example:

- Sequins, buttons, beads, shells, dried beans, and seeds
- String, wool, ribbon, and embroidery thread
- Nails, screws, paper clips, and washers

Sequins

Glue

Take care!

Some projects involve cutting, gluing, or spraying. Always ask an adult for help when you see this sign.

Frame it!

Choose your best work to frame in a simple or decorated card border. Start your own gallery!

Tools and brushes

Ordinary brushes are useful for backgrounds and details, but you might also want some unusual tools. Straws are good for blowing paint and for making paper quills. Toothpicks are good for scratchboard pictures.

Loom weaving

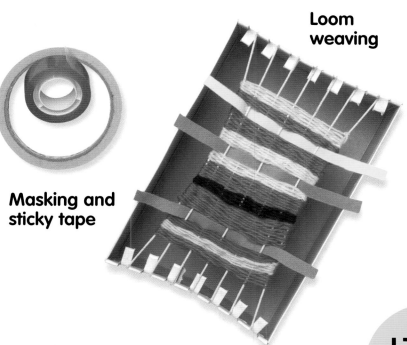

Masking and sticky tape

"Me" collage

Tell a story about yourself through a collage. The **theme** could be a birthday, a favorite hobby, or a vacation. How about a collage that tells people about your favorite things?

Top tip
Always ask an adult for help with cutting and gluing.

Soccer collage ideas
A soccer collage could include:
- Team photos
- Scraps from a soccer program
- Ticket stubs from a game
- Newspaper headlines about soccer stars
- Fabric from an old soccer shirt
- Shoelaces or cleats

You will need:
- Materials for your collage
- Cardboard or posterboard

1 Collect lots of things that tell a story. If you're not sure what to do, look at the pink and orange boxes on these pages for ideas.

2 Arrange all the things you have collected on a cardboard **mount board**. Move them around until you are happy with the way they look.

3 Glue down all the things to your piece of mount board with white glue. Glue a small area at a time.

Click for Art!

To see a photocollage by David Hockney, go to **http://artlex.com** and search for "photocollage."

Here's a fun collage made from ticket stubs, postcards, and other vacation souvenirs.

Vacation collage ideas

- Photographs from travel brochures or magazines
- Ticket stubs and luggage tags
- A sprinkling of sand and shells
- Food and candy wrappers
- Postcards and stamps
- Foreign coins

179

Magazine collage

Make a collage from scraps cut or torn from magazines. Choose a theme you find interesting—this one is about food. Look at the collage themes box for other ideas.

Collage themes

- Animals
- Ballet
- Cars
- Colors
- Dinosaurs
- Dogs
- Faces
- Flowers
- Happiness
- Horse riding
- Robots
- Space
- Sports
- Winter

You will need:

- Plenty of old newspapers and magazines
- Cardboard or posterboard

1 Find pictures in magazines about your theme. Using safety scissors, cut out as many pictures as you can.

2 Arrange the pictures on your mount board until you like the way they look.

3 Glue the pictures onto the mount board.

Click for Art!

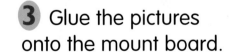

To see collages by Picasso, go to **www.tate.org.uk**, click on "Tate Collection," and find Picasso in "Artists A–Z."

3-D pictures

To make a picture stand out from the cardboard mount:

1 Glue the picture onto lightweight cardboard. Cut out around the picture.

2 Fold a strip of cardboard in half, then in half again. Open it out a little, so it looks like a chair with the bottom folded under.

3 Glue the flat part at the top to the mount board.

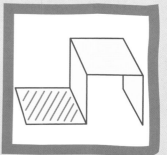

4 Glue the picture to the raised part that sticks out at the front.

This food collage uses pictures cut from magazines.

Paper collage

You can use all kinds of paper in a collage. Collect plain colored paper, construction paper, wrapping paper, wallpaper, candy wrappers, tissue paper, and newspaper.

Paper parrot

You will need:
- Different colors and textures of paper for the collage
- Cardboard or posterboard

Top tip
Try using layers of colored tissue papers so the top color mixes with the color below.

1 Plan your picture. Draw the picture lightly with a pencil on the mount board.

This parrot has been made from different kinds of paper that were cut into shapes and then glued in place.

Click for Art!

To see a collage by Henri Matisse, go to **www.tate.org.uk**. Click on "Tate Collection," then search "Matisse/The Snail."

2 Using safety scissors, cut out the different kinds of paper into the shapes you want for each part of the picture.

3 Move the pieces of paper around on your mount board until you like the way everything looks.

4 Glue down the paper shapes one at a time. To overlap shapes, glue larger pieces first, then smaller ones on top.

Fish shapes cut from foil

Tissue paper strips for seaweed

Sandy ocean floor cut from sandpaper

Collage face

The collage face on page 185 was made from cardboard that was cut, folded, and rolled in different ways.

There are lots of ways to make cardboard into different shapes.

The collage face on page 185 was made from cardboard that was cut, folded, and rolled in different ways.

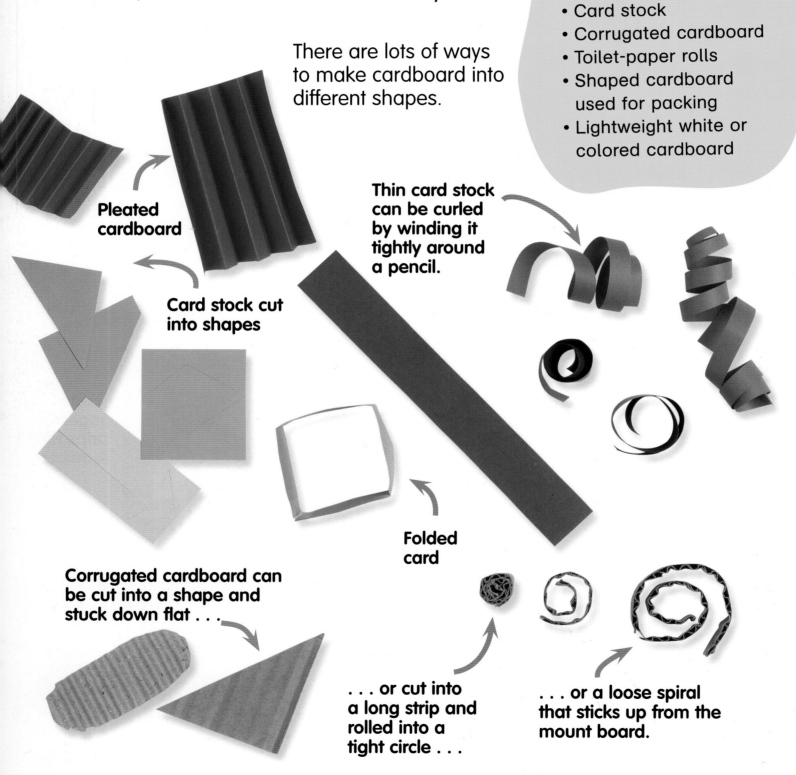

Cardboard crazy!

How many types of cardboard can you find? Try collecting:

- Empty food boxes
- Card stock
- Corrugated cardboard
- Toilet-paper rolls
- Shaped cardboard used for packing
- Lightweight white or colored cardboard

Pleated cardboard

Card stock cut into shapes

Thin card stock can be curled by winding it tightly around a pencil.

Folded card

Corrugated cardboard can be cut into a shape and stuck down flat . . .

. . . or cut into a long strip and rolled into a tight circle . . .

. . . or a loose spiral that sticks up from the mount board.

184

Life-size body collage

Ask a friend to lie down on a long piece of paper and draw around him or her with a pencil. Lightly draw in the face. Glue down lots of different materials, such as yarn, fabric, felt, torn paper, sequins, or ribbons, to make the face and clothes.

Hair made of thin green card stock, rolled into spirals

Eyes made of tightly rolled corrugated cardboard

Cardboard glued in wavy lines to make the mouth

Earrings made of pleated card stock

185

Food collage

It's fun to mix different materials and objects in a collage. Here's how to make a picture from scrap materials you may find around your home.

You will need:
- Dried food (see box)
- Black paper
- Cardboard for the mount board
- White or yellow pencil
- Tweezers

1 Glue the black paper onto a strong piece of cardboard as a mount board.

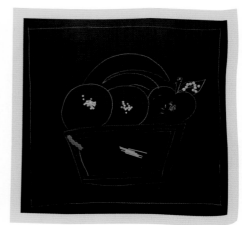

2 Plan your picture on a piece of white paper first. When you are happy with it, draw it onto the black paper with a white or yellow pencil.

3 Choose dried foods for the different parts of your picture. Sprinkle a few beans, lentils, or seeds in each area to remind you what goes where.

Food collage ideas

Food collages work best if you choose a simple pattern or picture. For example:

★ Flower
★ Tiger
★ Lizard
★ Snake with a zigzag pattern on its back

Top tip

To avoid sticky fingers and messy patches of glue, use tweezers to position items on your collage.

Food collage with border made from pasta wheels

5 Leave the collage flat until the glue has dried completely.

4 Spread glue thickly over a small part of the picture. Sprinkle small seeds over the glue.

Dried foods
★ Red and green lentils
★ Dried beans and peas
★ Pasta shapes and spaghetti
★ Black, white, and brown rice
★ Sunflower and poppy seeds
★ Pine nuts

187

Fabric collage

Collages made from different fabrics are great to look at—and to touch!

Collecting fabrics

Look for fabrics with different textures, such as scratchy burlap, smooth silk, and soft furs. Buy leftover pieces from stores or garage sales, or cut up old clothes—but always check with an adult first!

You will need:
- Scraps of fabric
- Wide-eyed needle and thread (optional)
- Thick cloth or cardboard for the mount board

Working with fabrics

You can use fabrics in a similar way to paper:

- Pleating: Glue the fabric down as you pleat it, or tack it with big, rough stitches using a needle and thread.

- Scrunching: Crumple the fabric and glue it down.

- Twisting: Twist the fabric, then glue it in place.

- Braiding: Braid strands of different fabrics into one.

- Cutting: Cut fabric into shapes to stick onto another material, or cut holes so you can see through to the fabric below.

I Plan your picture and draw it lightly onto the mount board.

Click for Art!

To see fabrics used in a collage, go to
www.wetcanvas.com/Articles2/4220/289/page5.php.

2 Using safety scissors, cut the fabric into shapes.

3 Arrange the shapes on the mount board until you are happy with the way they look. See the pink box for ways of giving your collage an interesting 3-D effect.

4 Glue down the shapes, one small area at a time.

Top tip
If you don't want the edges of your cloth to fray, cut your fabric with pinking shears to give the fabric a zigzag edge.

Flowers made from scrunched-up scraps of brightly colored fabric

Clouds made from scraps of netting and lace

Sheep's soft coats made from wool

Nature sculpture

Have fun making outdoor sculptures from smooth stones, fallen flowers and leaves, twigs, moss, or feathers. You can find all the things you need for free in parks, woods, fields, or your own yard!

Sculpture tips

Natural materials can make great outdoor sculptures. Here are some ideas to start you off:

- Arrange berries in a pattern on moss.
- Overlap fallen leaves in the shape of a circle or a star.
- Arrange flower petals on a stone or rock.
- Make rows of pebbles or shells on the beach.
- If it's been snowing, make a sculpture out of snow.

If it's been raining, trace lines in mud with a sharp stone or twig, then add a pattern of fallen leaves.

A spiral of tiny pebbles on a flat stone

Changing nature

Ask a grown-up to photograph your nature sculpture. Go back to it the next day and take another photograph to show how it has been changed by wind, rain, or animals.

Click for Art!

To see nature sculptures by Andy Goldsworthy, go to **www.sculpture.org.uk/image/000000100091**.

Colorful petals and leaves on grass

Shells arranged in the shape of a star

Thumb pot

This project shows you how to make a simple clay pot and decorate it with lively colors and patterns.

You will need:
- Air-drying clay
- Modeling tools

Add simple shapes like this star to decorate your pot.

1 Roll the clay into a ball between the palms of your hands. It should be about half the size of a tennis ball.

2 Holding the ball in one hand, push the thumb of your other hand into the middle of the clay.

3 Open out the middle of the pot by gently pinching the sides between your thumb and fingers. Keep turning the pot as you pinch, to keep the sides the same thickness.

4 When you like the pot's shape, flatten the bottom by tapping it gently on a flat surface. Let it dry out a little, then decorate it using modeling tools, or by adding pieces of clay.

Click for Art!

To see examples of clay pottery, go to **www.thebritishmuseum.ac.uk/compass** and search for "clay pot."

Top tip

In step 2, don't press down too hard with your thumb or you'll make a hole in the bottom of your pot!

Decorating your pot

When your clay pot is almost dry, decorate it with a **relief pattern** or press patterns into the side with modeling tools. If you don't have special pottery tools, use:

★ The tip of a pen or pencil
★ A large nail
★ The end of a ruler
★ A blunt metal knife or fork

5 When the clay is completely hard, paint your pot with poster paint and let it dry. Finish it off with a coat of craft glue mixed with a little water.

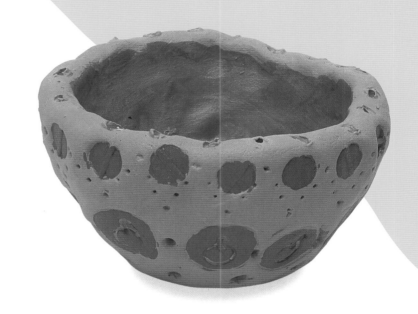

"Studs" made from flattened balls of clay

Long, thin snakes of clay stuck on with a little water

193

Aztec monkey pot

Make a clay pot using the same coil technique as the Aztecs. The monkey god Ozomatli (oh-zoh-maht-lee) protected art, games, and fun.

Buyers and sellers hoped to get a good deal at the market.

You will need:
- Air-drying clay
- Modeling tools
- Black acrylic paint
- Paintbrushes

Aztec traders brought this monkey pot from the city of Texcoco to sell. It is carved from shiny black obsidian (a stone produced by erupting volcanoes).

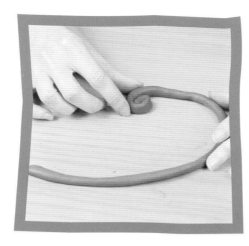

1 Shape the clay into balls. Then use your hands to roll out the balls into several long, thin "sausages."

2 Fold in one end of the first sausage and then coil the rest around and around to build up the pot.

3 If you need to add another sausage, just blend the end on. When the pot is big enough, smooth the sides.

4 Roll a dime-size ball of clay for the head and four small sausages for the feet. Shape the head and feet.

5 Attach the head and feet to the pot and smooth the joins. When the clay has dried, paint it black.

To make your pot shine, use a clean brush to add a layer of glue mixture (mix three parts white school glue to one part water).

Roman plaque

Practice your Latin by making a Roman plaque for your bedroom door. Inscribe it with "Salvete amici," which means "Greetings, friends!"

A portrait of a Roman woman writing poetry. She is using a pointed stick, called a stylus, to write on a wax-covered tablet.

You will need:

- Air-drying clay
- Rolling pin
- Ruler
- Plastic knife
- Modeling tool
- Pencil
- Paint and paintbrushes
- Length of string

Pupils and scribes jotted down notes on wax-covered tablets like this one.

I Roll out a ½-inch-thick slab of clay. Use a plastic knife to cut out a 6 x 3-inch rectangle.

2 With a modeling tool, draw a ¾-inch border. In the center of the plaque, inscribe your Latin message.

Did you Know?
Many languages still contain Latin words. Castle, memory, monster, mile, plumber, triumph, ultimate, and extraordinary all come from Latin.

3 Add pieces of clay to build up the border. With a sharp pencil, make a hole in each of the top corners.

4 When your tablet is completely dry, paint it using Roman colors such as black, red, and white.

Copy the Roman-style letters shown here to make your plaque as realistic as possible.

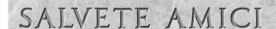

SALVETE AMICI

5 Once the paint is dry, thread the string through both holes, tie the ends together, and hang it up.

Aztec rain god pendant

Aztec jewelry designs often featured gods. Make a pendant of Tlaloc, the god of rain and good harvests, in a few simple steps.

You will need:

- Air-drying clay
- Rolling pin
- Tracing paper
- Pencil
- Scissors
- Modeling tool
- Acrylic paints
- Paintbrushes
- String

The rain god Tlaloc (tlah-lock) was known as "He Who Makes Things Grow." The Aztecs worshipped him because there would be no crops unless the rains came.

Did you know?

Human excrement made excellent manure to help crops grow. Farmers collected the excrement from public toilets!

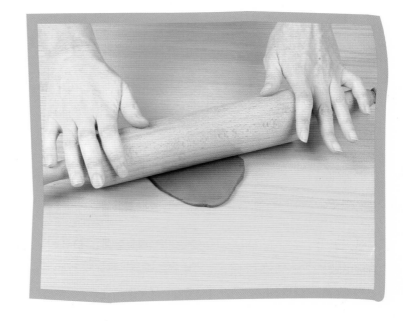

1 Warm the clay in your hands for a few moments and then roll out a slab that's about ½ inch thick.

2 Trace the image of Tlaloc from the opposite page. Cut your tracing out and place it on the clay.

3 With a modeling tool, cut around your tracing. Cut zigzags along the top to make his crown.

4 Use a pencil to make two eye holes right through the clay. Add his nose, mouth, and teeth.

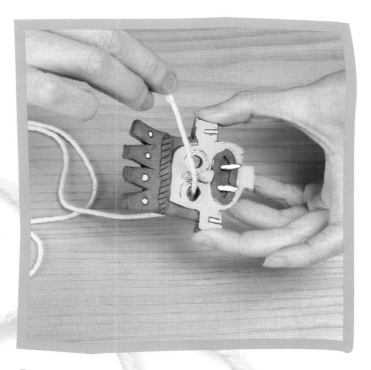

5 When your pendant is dry, paint it in bright colors. Once the paint is dry, thread string through the eyes.

Wear your pendant and watch for rain!

Thor's hammer

Viking blacksmiths poured molten metal into molds to make objects in special shapes. You can do the same with plaster of Paris!

Viking men and women liked to carry amulets (lucky charms). Many were shaped like the magic hammer used by the god Thor when he fought giants and monsters.

You will need:

- Nondrying clay
- Ruler
- Modeling tools
- Old pen top
- Plaster of Paris mixture (always follow the instructions on the packet)

A little metal statue of the goddess Freya. Vikings said she made people, animals, and plants grow strong and healthy.

Did you Know?

Some days of the week are named after Viking gods, such as Thursday, which means "Thor's day."

1 Shape nondrying clay into a small block. Press the sides against a ruler to make them smooth and straight.

2 With a modeling tool, scoop out the hammer shape. Be careful not to go through the bottom!

3 Press a pen top into the bottom of your mold to make circle patterns on your hammer.

4 Following the instructions on the packet, mix up the plaster of Paris. Pour it up to the top of the mold.

5 When the plaster of Paris has completely dried, carefully peel away the clay mold to reveal your amulet.

You could use gold or silver paint to make your amulet look like metal.

Clay sculpture

People have been making clay models for thousands of years. For this project, you can use air-drying modeling clay, so you don't need to fire it in a **kiln**.

You will need:
- Air-drying clay
- Modeling tools

1 Tear off a piece of clay and work it into the shape of a head with your fingers.

2 Add features by sticking on extra pieces of clay or cutting away areas. Make hair by rolling the clay into strands.

3 Stop when you're happy with how your model looks, and let the clay harden.

Top tip
Coat your finished model with glue mixed with a little water. The glue looks white at first, but dries to a clear, shiny finish.

4 Paint your model with poster paints and let it dry.

Click for Art!

To see sculptures by Henry Moore, go to **www.henry-moore-fdn.co.uk**. Click on the link to "Perry Green," then on the interactive map, then on photos of sculptures.

Animal shapes

Here are some simple animal shapes made out of clay.

203

Junk robot

You can make fantastic sculptures out of scrap materials! This robot has been made from cardboard boxes and tubes spray painted silver.

You will need:
- A large cardboard box
- Smaller boxes for the robot's lower body, hands, and feet
- 7 toilet-paper tubes
- **Corrugated cardboard**
- Silver spray paint

1 Glue down the open top of a cardboard box. Ask an adult to help you make a hole in the top and push in a toilet-paper tube for the robot's neck. Secure it with sticky tape.

2 Glue on a smaller cardboard box to make the lower part of the robot's body. Make two holes underneath and attach toilet-paper tubes for the legs.

3 Tape two toilet-paper tubes together to make each of the robot's arms. Secure them to the sides of the robot's body with craft glue.

Click for Art! To see Picasso's "Head of a Bull," a sculpture made with a bicycle seat and handlebars, go to **www.artviews.org/cosby.htm** and scroll down.

Top tip

For a shiny, metallic look, ask an adult to help you spray paint your robot silver.

4 Cut out the ears, eyes, and a mouth from cardboard and glue them to a small cardboard box to make the robot's head.

5 Ask an adult to help you cut a hole in the bottom of the head and attach it to the robot's neck.

6 Glue on feet made from small cardboard boxes. Paint the robot when the glue is dry.

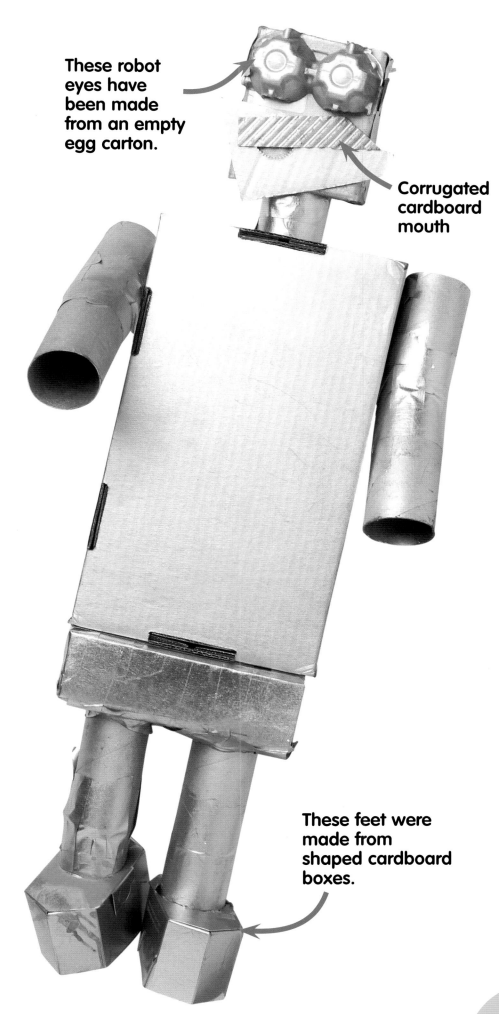

These robot eyes have been made from an empty egg carton.

Corrugated cardboard mouth

These feet were made from shaped cardboard boxes.

Paper sculpture

This colorful bird has been made out of different kinds of paper that have been folded, creased, or curled to look three-dimensional.

You will need:
- Colored construction paper
- Scrunched-up newspaper
- Ribbon or yarn
- Stapler

Bird of paradise

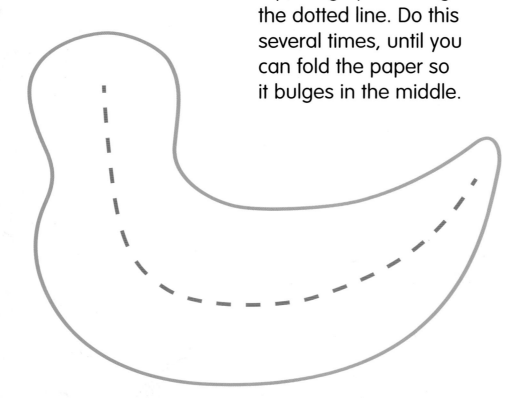

1 Ask an adult to help you copy and enlarge the bird shape below onto two sheets of brightly colored paper.

2 Cut out one of the shapes and crease it with a ballpoint pen top, roughly following the dotted line. Do this several times, until you can fold the paper so it bulges in the middle.

3 Do the same with the other shape, but crease it on the opposite side.

4 Ask an adult to help you staple the two pieces of paper together so the sides bulge out. Leave a gap at the bird's head and tail, then stuff it with scrunched-up pieces of newspaper.

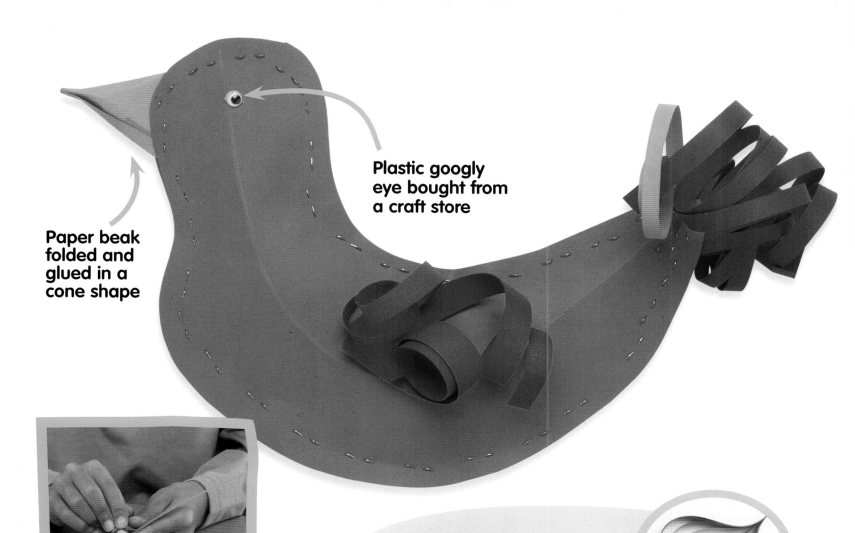

Paper beak folded and glued in a cone shape

Plastic googly eye bought from a craft store

5 Using safety scissors, cut out thin strips of colored paper and wind them tightly around a pen or pencil so they curl.

6 Glue long, brightly colored paper curls to make the bird's tail, and shorter curls for the wings.

7 Hang the finished sculpture on the wall with a length of ribbon or yarn.

paper decorations

1 Cut out six to ten strips of paper about 1 inch wide.

2 Leave two strips 12 inches long. Cut two strips 11 inches long, and cut two more strips 10 inches long.

3 Arrange the strips with the long ones on the outside and the shorter ones in the middle.

4 Staple the strips together at the top and bottom so the shape balloons out, then hang it up.

Cone hats

These cute hats are great to make—and fun to wear!

1 Ask an adult to help you draw a big circle on a sheet of cardboard and cut it out with safety scissors. Cut a straight line from the edge of the circle to the exact center.

2 Overlap the edges to make a cone shape that fits your head, then secure the edges together with glue or tape.

3 Paint your hat and decorate it with ribbons, sequins, or glitter.

4 Ask an adult to help you make a hole in each side of the hat. Cut a piece of elastic or ribbon and tie it through the holes.

You will need:

- Large sheet of cardboard
- Ribbons, sequins, stick-on gems, glitter, and feathers for decoration
- Elastic or ribbon

Click for Art!

To see sculptural hats designed by Pip Hackett, go to **www.vam.ac.uk/collections/fashion** and search for "Pip Hackett."

Wizard's hat

Moons and stars cut from foil

Animal ears

1 Using safety scissors, cut out a strip of cardboard 2 inches wide, and long enough to go around your head plus an extra 1 inch.

2 Fit the strip around your head, and then ask an adult to staple the ends of the cardboard together.

3 Cut out animal ear shapes from cardboard and glue them to the band.

Rabbit ears painted with poster paints

Top tip
Try cutting out different sizes of circles. The bigger the circle, the wider or taller the hat. The wizard's hat was made from a circle 39 inches wide.

Pyramid

Make a gleaming gold-and-white pyramid from card stock. Once you've finished, you can hide your own treasures deep inside the pyramid!

Three of the greatest Egyptian pyramids, at Giza. They were originally covered with slabs of white limestone and tipped with real gold.

You will need:

- White card stock
- Ruler
- Pencil
- Craft knife
- Scissors
- Double-sided tape
- Gold paint and a paintbrush, or a gold paint pen

1 Draw a triangle with 5-inch sides on card stock. Ask an adult to cut it out with a craft knife and ruler.

2 Place the triangle on a big sheet of card and trace it. Line it up beside the first outline and trace it again.

3 Draw two more triangles using the same method. Now draw on a ¼-inch tab, as shown.

These tomb wall paintings show the kingdom of Osiris, the Egyptian god who helped the dead make the journey into the afterlife.

4 Cut around the outer edge of your shape. Ask an adult to score along all the inner lines.

Did you know?

The most famous rock tombs are in Egypt's Valley of the Kings, near Thebes. King Tutankhamen was buried there in 1352 BC, surrounded by treasures.

5 Color the tip of the pyramid gold using paint or gold pen. Add lines to show the limestone panels.

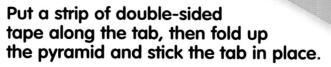

Put a strip of double-sided tape along the tab, then fold up the pyramid and stick the tab in place.

Ocean scene

First make and decorate this box for a **3-D** ocean scene—then turn the page to find out how to fill it with fish and other sea creatures!

1 Cut off the flaps on the open side of the box, or fold them back and glue them to the sides.

3 Glue a piece of blue cellophane underneath the hole in the top of the box to create a watery blue light.

You will need:

- A large cardboard box
- Blue cellophane
- Newspaper
- Sandpaper, pebbles, and shells

2 Ask an adult to help you cut a rectangular hole in the top of the box to let in light at the back. Paint the box blue inside and out.

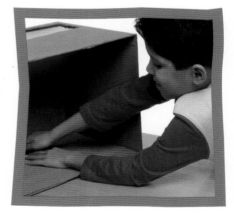

4 Glue sandpaper, small pebbles, and shells onto the bottom of your box to make a sandy seabed.

Click for Art!

To see the outdoor sculptures of Claes Oldenburg and Coosje van Bruggen, go to www.metmuseum.org/explore/oldenburg/artist.html.

5 Scrunch up some old newspaper and pack it tightly into a corner of your box. Secure it in place with tape and glue.

6 Tear more newspaper into strips and glue two or three layers over the scrunched-up newspaper, overlapping them as you go.

7 When the glue is dry, paint the newspaper brown or gray, for rocks.

Now turn the page to find out how to make the sea creatures to put in the box.

Ocean creatures

Now that you've made the box for your **3-D** ocean scene, it's time to fill it with colorful fish and sea creatures.

You will need:
• Air-drying clay
• Plastic bottle
• Glitter glue
• Clear plastic food bag
• Tissue paper
• Transparent nylon fishing line

Clay crab and fishes

Use air-drying clay to make these sea creatures for your ocean scene.

Have fun decorating your models with bright colors and spotted patterns!

Plastic bottle fish

These fish were cut out of a large plastic bottle, then painted with wavy and zigzag patterns.

Ask an adult to make a hole at the top of your fish, so you can hang it from the top of your box with nylon fishing line.

This sea snail was made from colored air-drying clay.

This sea horse was made from cardboard, built up with layers of glued newspaper strips, and then painted.

plastic-bag jellyfish

1 Push some colorful scrunched-up tissue paper into a clear plastic food bag.

2 Tie the bag around the middle, then cut the open end into strips for the jellyfish's tentacles.

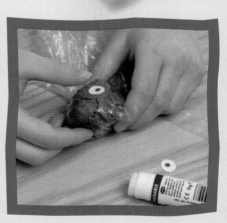

3 Glue on some big cardboard eyes or some googly eyes from a craft store.

Click for Art!

To design a 3-D shape on an interactive art site, go to **www.nga.gov/kids/zone/zone.htm** and click on "3-D Twirler." You may have to download a program to work it.

215

Special paint effects

You can give your paintings an extra twist by adding glitter or cornstarch to paint, or sprinkling salt onto wet paint.

You will need:
- Glitter
- Cornstarch
- Soft, wide paintbrush
- Salt crystals

1 Wet the paper all over by applying water with a soft, wide brush.

2 While the paper is wet, drip blobs of paint in a circle and let them spread.

3 Add a tiny dot of paint for the center of each flower. Sprinkle grains of salt over the painted petals. Watch how the salt soaks up the paint and makes speckled marks on the paper.

Flower painting

When the paint is dry, add stems for the flowers with a thin brush.

Click for Art!

For a good art Web site that includes art galleries, art quizzes, and information about artists and their work, plus links to other art sites, visit **www.scribbleskidsart.com**.

Top tip

Shake off the salt when the paint is dry, or leave it on if you want more texture in your painting.

All that glitters

It's easy to make your own sparkly glitter paint. Just add glitter to acrylic or poster paint and paint it on with a brush as usual.

Adding texture

To thicken poster paint, add a few spoonfuls of cornstarch. Keep mixing until you have the texture you want. Paint with a brush as usual. If you like, make patterns in the paint with a stick or comb.

Wax resist

Waxy crayons and watery paints don't mix—which means that if you draw a picture in crayon and then paint over the top, the drawing will show through.

You will need:
- White wax crayon
- Paper
- Poster paints

1 Use the wax crayon to draw the **outline** of the squash and add some lines running along it.

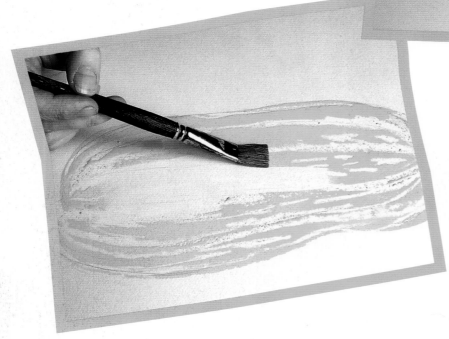

2 Brush yellow paint over the wax. The wax will **resist** the paint and the lines will show through.

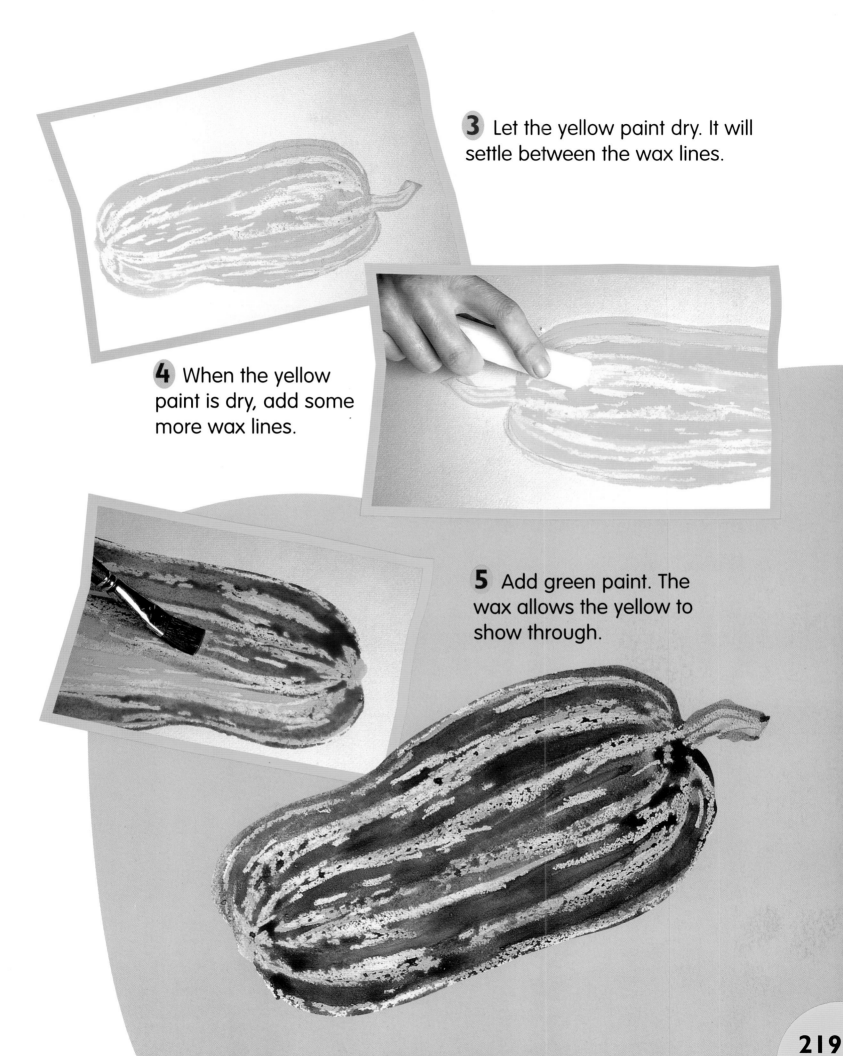

3 Let the yellow paint dry. It will settle between the wax lines.

4 When the yellow paint is dry, add some more wax lines.

5 Add green paint. The wax allows the yellow to show through.

Scratchboard

While watery paints slide off wax crayon, you can get quite different results if you cover the whole area with thick paint, and then scratch patterns on the surface.

You will need:

- Heavyweight paper or posterboard
- Crayons or a candle
- Poster paint
- Paintbrushes

Make your own scratchboard

1 Cover the paper with crayon, without any gaps. Whatever color you use will show through—so choose bright colors or use a white candle.

2 Now brush thick black paint over the crayon surface, and let it dry. Repeat two or three times until the crayon is completely covered.

Making pictures

3 Scrape a pattern in the surface, using various tools—try the end of a paintbrush, a Popsicle stick, or even a knitting needle.

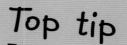

Top tip

Experiment with different scratchboard techniques. Instead of covering the crayon with black paint, use dark crayons and then cover them with white paint—black showing through white is very dramatic.

Top tip

You could also try making lots of small scratchboard pictures rather than one large one. Try using lots of different colors of crayons— diagonal lines of red and orange make great flickering flame effects.

Wax transfer

You can use wax crayons to make homemade transfers. Try out some simple designs, such as flower shapes, and after you have practiced this technique, you can make more detailed, colorful pictures.

You will need:
- Crayons
- Paper
- Pencil

1 Cover part of a piece of paper with crayon. Lay a clean piece of paper on top.

2 Draw a simple design on top of the paper with the pencil. Fill it in, pressing hard.

3 Lift off the paper. The crayon should have transferred to the underside of the top piece of paper, leaving a pale copy on the piece below.

Color transfer

Using this wax transfer effect, you can turn a simple **silhouette** into an unusual, colorful picture.

You will need:
- Parchment paper
- Heavyweight paper
- Crayons
- Pencil

1 Lightly draw or trace a design on one side of the parchment paper. You don't need to keep the shapes simple.

2 Turn the parchment paper over, and color it with different colors of crayons. Try bands of color, splotches, circles, or squares.

3 Place the parchment paper, crayon-side down, on a clean sheet of paper. Tape the edges so it doesn't slip. Now go over all the lines and areas of solid color with the pencil, pressing firmly.

4 Lift off the parchment paper to see the wax transfer beneath.

223

Glitter project

Glitter comes in lots of different colors and can be used to make wonderful, sparkling pictures. Try this rocket idea.

Paint and sparkle

In this project, you use glue like paint to draw the shapes you want in your picture. Before the glue is dry, add some sparkle!

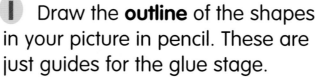

You will need:
- Colored paper
- Pencil
- Glitter
- Glue
- Paintbrush

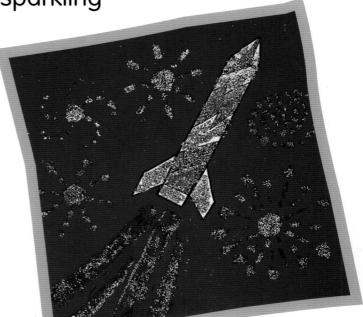

Try making this rocket picture first. Then think of some other pictures that would look good in glitter.

1 Draw the **outline** of the shapes in your picture in pencil. These are just guides for the glue stage.

2 Use the brush to paint glue into your shapes. You could just use blobs or fill in the shapes.

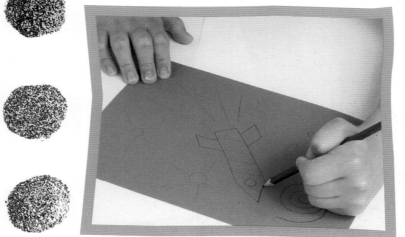

3 Before the glue dries, pick up some glitter and sprinkle it onto the picture. Use different-colored glitters for different areas so the finished picture is bright. Leave the glitter on for a few minutes before lightly shaking off the extra glitter. The rest will have stuck to the glue and made a colorful image.

Top tip

You can make your own glitter paint. Just mix some glitter with some glue and use a brush to put the sparkly paint on your paper. Now you can make your own glittering masterpieces.

Material world

You can make fantastic pictures using fabric. Think about different looks and textures when choosing your materials. For example, cotton balls make good fluffy clouds, or you could use lace for a more interesting effect. Have fun as you create your own country scene.

1 First, sketch the **outline** of the scene on your paper in soft pencil. It is best to use cardboard because normal paper might tear.

2 Cut out the large **background** pieces of fabric. You'll need blue for the sky, dark green for hills, and light green for the fields.

3 Now start adding all the details: a fence, a hedge, trees, animals in the fields, clouds, and some flowers.

Top tip
Collect old bits of fabric for your pictures. Scraps of white lace are excellent for making clouds or for snowy scenes. Ribbons are handy for creating flowers. Try experimenting with different fabrics for different objects.

Top tip
When you have finished your fabric **collage**, you can paint it with clear **varnish**. This adds depth and makes the surface of the picture shine. The varnish effect looks great on a dark background.

Paper sewing

Sewing isn't just for fabric. You can also use your needle and thread to make great designs on paper or cardboard. Always ask an adult for help when you want to use a needle. You could even use sewing in one of your paintings!

You will need:
- Posterboard
- Plain paper
- Needle
- **Embroidery** thread
- Adhesive tape
- Glue

Embroidery house

This simple project will show you the basic method of paper sewing. Try some other designs.

1 Draw a simple design on paper. Tape it over the posterboard, and sew thread through the paper and into the board. Discard the paper.

2 On the back of the posterboard, neaten the loose threads. Knot the ends, cut the excess, and put small pieces of tape over the joins.

3 Finally, cut another piece of posterboard slightly larger than the one with the sewing on it. Glue the sewing picture onto this.

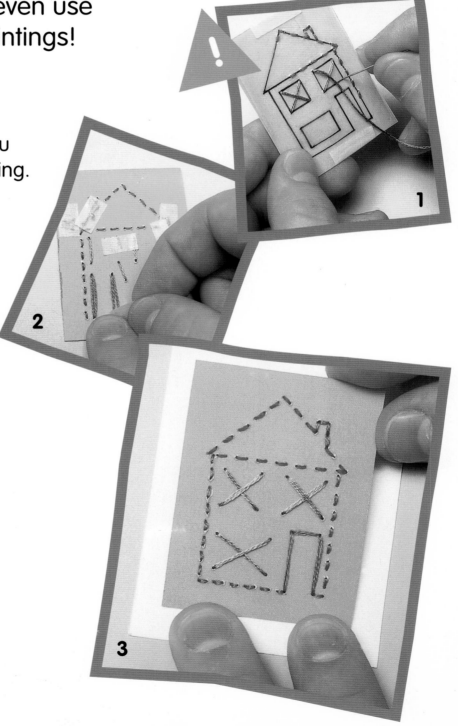

Stitching decorations

There are lots of variations you can use with paper sewing. Try putting colorful beads onto the thread and making zigzag patterns. You can use thread to make decorative borders on your cards and letters—just make sure you use paper thick enough to hold the thread.

Paper pricking

You could also just use the needle to make holes in the paper that show up when light shines through them. This is a technique called paper pricking.

Top tip

See if you can use sewing in some of your paintings or **collages**. You could use thread to make hair, colorful plants in the garden, or even a waterfall. Use different colors of thread together to get interesting results.

Top tip

In addition to decorative borders, you can use sewing to make colorful designs for birthday and holiday cards. Using the same method as the project on page 228, you can make any shape or design you like.

Collage

Paper and cardboard are cheap, colorful, and easy to cut and paste, which makes them perfect for **collage.** Keep as many scraps as you can find—you never know when they may come in handy!

You will need:
• Colored paper or magazines
• Posterboard or cardboard
• Glue

Making a collage

1 Sketch out a design on cardboard or posterboard.

2 Cut or tear paper shapes to make up the design.

3 Arrange the shapes until you are happy with the way they look. Glue them in place.

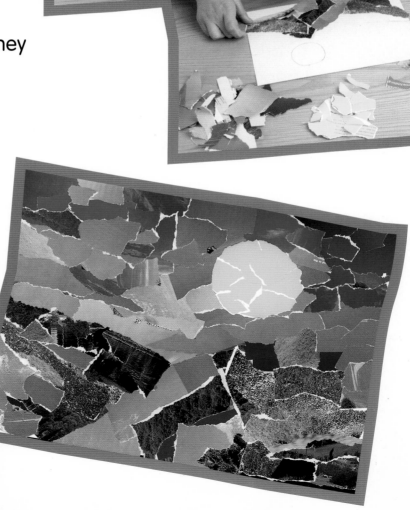

Mosaic

Try some different techniques in your collages. What about cutting out lots of small, colored squares from old magazines and making them into an image like a Roman **mosaic**?

Here is another colorful collage made with different types of paper.

Experiment with other materials, too, such as buttons, aluminum foil, and newspaper. You could also paint pieces of paper different colors, tear them up, and then use them in your collages. Torn paper creates interesting **textures**.

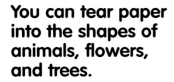

You can tear paper into the shapes of animals, flowers, and trees.

Top tip

Once you have used paper to make colorful **collages**, you can go on to make paper sculptures. Cut out the shapes you'll need for your design, then color them before you glue them together. You can make hair by cutting thin strips of paper.

You could even make a sculpture out of paper.

Bits and pieces

Scraps and remnants from around the home look great in **collages**: fabric, lace, ribbons, **sequins,** pasta, beans, and toothpicks. You could probably make a collage from the contents of your wastebasket!

You will need:
- Fluffy feathers
- String
- Toothpicks
- Colored paper
- Dry leaves
- Beads
- Rice
- Cardboard
- Glue

Perfect pets

1 Draw the **outlines** of your picture with a pen, then cut them out. Cut just inside the lines, so that the pen marks don't show—or turn your cut-out shapes the other way around.

2 Arrange the main shapes on the cardboard. When you are happy with the way they look, glue them down.

3 Now add a bead for the eye, rice for flowers, toothpicks and string for the fence, colored paper for the apples, and feathers for the mane and tail.

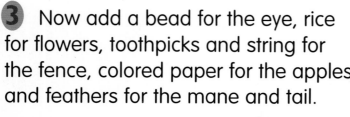

Still life

All the items used in this collage are easy to find. You can adapt it by mixing the collage with painting and adding other materials, such as dried beans, seeds, and pasta.

1 Think about how you could make what you've collected into a collage. Sketch the design on cardboard.

2 Arrange your collection on the pencil outline. Glue it in place.

3 You could leave your collage as it is, or paint in a **background** and some flowers among your collage flower heads. Try adding color to some of the objects in the collage if you like.

Using photos

A camera can be useful in art. You can get all kinds of unusual effects if you combine photos with painting and **collage**. Keep your eyes open for interesting shots, and save photographs from magazines.

Fantasy fun

1 Want a different home? Take a photo of your house and paint an unusual **background** to make it look as if you live somewhere else. Look in travel brochures for inspiration.

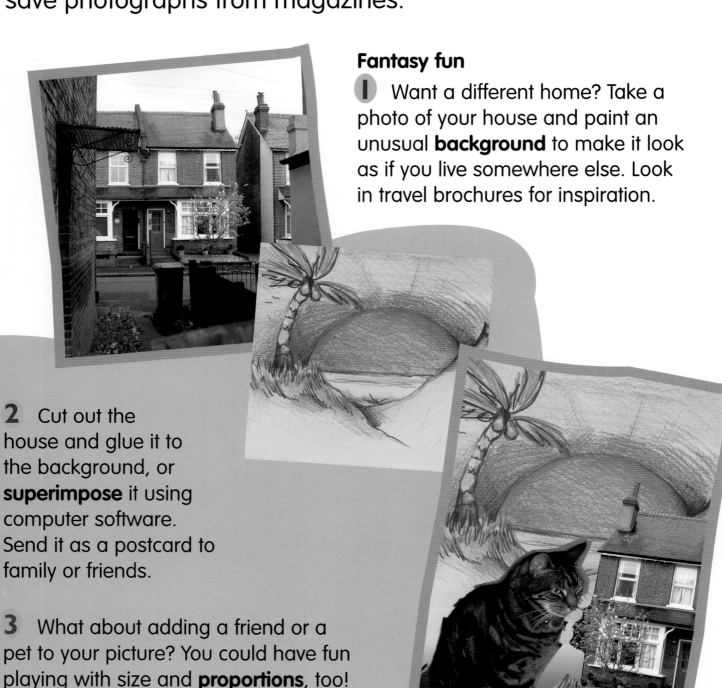

2 Cut out the house and glue it to the background, or **superimpose** it using computer software. Send it as a postcard to family or friends.

3 What about adding a friend or a pet to your picture? You could have fun playing with size and **proportions**, too! In your fantasy picture, objects can be as big or as small as you like.

Picture strips

1 Find two photos or magazine pictures, roughly the same size, and divide them into equal sections ¾ inch wide.

2 Cut along the lines to make neat strips.

3 Now glue the first strip from the first picture onto some cardboard, followed by the first strip from the second picture. Keep going, using a strip at a time from each picture, until you've used all the strips.

You can use this effect to mix different animals, or alternate an animal with a photo of a celebrity or a landscape.

Top tip
Try cutting the strips diagonally or horizontally for a different effect.

235

Glossary

abstract pictures that do not look like real objects

accordion fold folding a piece of paper or cardboard into small folds so that it has an accordion, or fanlike, shape

acrylic easy-to-mix paint that dries quickly and can be cleaned with soap and water

backdrop the scenery in a theater, at the back of the stage

background the area of a picture behind the main object

batik a way of decorating cloth using wax and colored dye

chalk a soft stick of rock used for making soft, smudgy pictures

charcoal a drawing tool made from charred wood

checkered having a pattern that is made up of squares

collage pictures or patterns made using different materials, such as paper and fabric, which are glued onto a background

complementary colors colors that work well together

construction paper a rough-textured paper—good for chalk and charcoal drawings

corrugated cardboard cardboard that has ridges in it

cube a shape with six square sides

Cubism a form of art in which pictures were made up from fragments of images

dye powder or liquid used to color something, usually cloth

embroidery making pictures or patterns with sewing

expressions the look on a person's face when he or she is happy, sad, angry, etc.

features parts of the face, such as the eyes, nose, and mouth, which make everyone look different

felt thick, fuzzy cloth

foreground the area at the front of a picture

frames boxes that make up a page in a comic book, or the borders of pictures

fungicide poison that is used to kill mold

geometric a pattern made up of regular shapes

highlights the bright parts of a picture

horizontal lines that run across the page from side to side

hues shades or tints of a particular color

kiln a large, hot oven used to fire clay to make it harden (air-drying clay doesn't need to be fired in a kiln)

landscape a scene such as a countryside showing trees and hills or a city skyline showing factories and buildings

latex paint a type of water-based paint, often used for painting walls

Matisse, Henri French artist (1869–1954)

Morris, William British artist and writer (1834–1896)

mosaic picture or pattern made up of lots of small squares of color

mount board a piece of cardboard or sturdy paper onto which things are stuck

mural a decorative painting on a wall

nib the writing end of a pen

outline the outer edge of an object—you usually draw these first and add the details later

palette a piece of wood or plastic used to mix paints in

pattern repetition of shape, line, or color in a design

Picasso, Pablo Spanish artist (1881–1973)

portfolio a case for storing and carrying your drawings

primary colors red, green, and blue—the colors that are mixed to make all other colors

proportion the relative size of one thing to another

relief when part of a pattern or picture sticks out from the background

resist to not accept something; wax resists paint, which means it shows through the paint

resist work a form of printing in which you cover a raised surface with ink or paint and then press this down on a sheet of paper

secondary colors the colors that are made by mixing primary colors

shade to color in part of your drawing to make that area darker

silhouette a solid picture that is done by drawing an outline and filling it in using one color

sketchbook a book that is used for making quick sketches that can be used as ideas for proper paintings or drawings

sketch paper very inexpensive paper—good for rough work, rather than finished drawings

stencil a shape cut out of cardboard, which can be painted through or around

superimpose to put one thing on top of another

symmetrical a shape that is the same on both sides

tapestry a heavy fabric picture or design made by weaving colored threads

texture the surface of something—some papers have a smooth texture, other papers have a rougher texture

theme the subject of something, such as an idea for a film

three-dimensional (3-D) when an object has (or appears to have) height, width, and depth

varnish clear paint that dries hard and protects the surface beneath it

vertical lines that run from the top to bottom of a page

Warhol, Andy American artist (1928–1987)

watercolors paints that mix with water; they are sold in tubes or blocks

Notes for parents and teachers

The projects in this book are suitable for use in the home or can be used as stand-alone lessons in the classroom. They can also be used to complement other areas of study.

While the ideas in the book are offered as inspiration, children should always be encouraged to paint, draw, sculpt, or create from their own imaginations and firsthand observations.

Sourcing ideas

All art projects should tap into children's interests, and be directly relevant to their lives and experiences. Try using stimulating starting points such as found objects, discussions about their family and pets, hobbies, TV programs, or favorite places.

Encourage children to source their own ideas and references from books, magazines, the Internet, or CD-ROM collections.

Digital cameras can be used to create reference material (pictures of landscapes, people, or animals) and can also be used in tandem with children's finished work (see below). .

Other lessons can often be an ideal springboard for an art project—for example, a geography field trip can be used as a source of ideas for a landscape picture.

Encourage children to keep a sketchbook to sketch ideas for future paintings and creations, and to collect other images and objects to help them develop their work.

Give children as many firsthand experiences as possible through visits and contact with creative people.

Evaluating work

Arrange for the children to share their work with others, and to compare ideas and methods—this is often very motivating. Encourage them to talk about their work.

Show the children examples of other artists' paintings, sculptures, etc.—how did they tackle the same subject and problems?

Help children to judge the originality and value of their creations, to appreciate the different qualities in others' work, and to value ways of working that are different from their own.

Going further

Look at ways of developing the projects further—for example, adapting the work into collage, print, or ceramics.

Use image-enhancing computer software and digital scanners to enhance, build up, and juxtapose images.

Show the children how to develop a class art gallery on their school's Web site.